DOROTHY RUBIN

Professor of Education
Trenton State College

The Teacher's Handbook of Reading/ Thinking Exercises

Holt, Rinehart and Winston
NEW YORK   CHICAGO   SAN FRANCISCO   DALLAS
MONTREAL   TORONTO   LONDON   SYDNEY

Acknowledgments: *P. 7,* excerpt from Herbert S. Zim, *Sharks.* Copyright © 1960 by Herbert S. Zim and Reprinted by permission of William Morrow & Company; *p. 8,* excerpt from George and Kay Schaller, *Wonder of Lions,* reprinted by permission of the publisher, Dodd, Mead & Company; *p. 9,* excerpt from Robert Trowbridge, "Fight Your Nightmares," *Cricket,* October 1978, p. 18. All of the excerpts first appeared in *Cricket* magazine.

Library of Congress Cataloging in Publication Data

Rubin, Dorothy.
   The teacher's handbook of reading/thinking exercises.

   1. Reading (Elementary)   2. Reading comprehension.
I.   Title
LB1573.R69   372.4   80–12837
ISBN 0-03-056122-1

Copyright © 1980 by Holt, Rinehart and Winston
All rights reserved
Printed in the United States of America

0 1 2   140   9 8 7 6 5 4 3 2 1

ABOUT THIS RESOURCE

Purpose

THE TEACHER'S HANDBOOK OF READING/THINKING EXER-CISES will be a valuable resource for you. It provides you with a wealth of challenging and stimulating **reading comprehension exercises** for your students. The wide variety of material contained in THE HANDBOOK will help you work easily with students of differing abilities. THE HANDBOOK is published in a format so that the **exercise material is easily reproducible** for distribution to the children in your class. THE HANDBOOK will be an important **time saver** for you. It will enable you to allow your students to work independently with material geared to each ability level.

The skills presented in THE TEACHER'S HANDBOOK OF READING/THINKING EXERCISES are those dealing with word meanings and reasoning with verbal concepts because these are the two major abilities that comprise reading comprehension. Comprehension involves thinking. As there are various levels in the hierarchy of thinking so are there various levels of comprehension. Higher levels of comprehension would obviously include higher levels of thinking. This book concentrates on the higher level comprehension skills because these are often neglected in schools, and all students need help in acquiring these skills. Also many reading task forces across the country are emphasizing the teaching of higher level comprehension skills.

Who It's For

The exercises are designed primarily for students in the intermediate grades and above. If you are a teacher with gifted students below the intermediate-grade level, you will also find THE HANDBOOK an especially good teaching tool. It provides the kind of challenge in higher level thinking skills that gifted children need.

Some Suggestions for Use

THE HANDBOOK can be used in a number of ways and with a variety of audiences. Criterion-referenced tests can be used to diagnose specific reading behaviors of individual students. This information can be used to either reinforce, supplement, enrich, or remediate the skill development area being tested using material from THE HANDBOOK. You can either choose the needed exercises for individual students and provide the students with these exercises, or you can send the student to the reading learning center.

The materials in each section of THE HANDBOOK can be used to stock a reading learning center because exercises with clear directions, objectives, and answers are given for each skill. In doing this you can have the students working individually and then go over the answers in a group to allow for an interaction of ideas. Of course, you can do the same for any skill with any group of students.

After students have had an opportunity to work on a number of the word puzzles or riddles in the "Fun With Words" section of the book, you can go over these with the whole class. To make sure that everyone has had an opportunity to work on these, a schedule can be posted stating which puzzles or riddles will be gone over on a specific day.

The exercises in THE HANDBOOK also lend themselves very well to programs using management learning systems because in THE HANDBOOK the specific skill being developed is given as well as the objectives, exercises, and answers.

Organization

THE HANDBOOK is organized into two parts. Part I, "Exercise Material and Activities for Your Students" is divided into the following sections:

Section One: Selected Reading/Thinking Skills
Section Two: Vocabulary Expansion Skills
Section Three: Fun With Words: Word Riddles and Word
                 Puzzles

Sections One and Two contain **thirteen skill areas and a total of 134 exercises**. Each skill is introduced and clear and understandable directions are provided for each skill. A couple of practice exercises (with answers) follow. After the directions you will then find **up to twenty exercises for each skill area**. The exercises in each skill are graduated in levels of difficulty. The beginning exercises are easier and the following ones are more difficult. You can, therefore, choose the exercises based on the ability level of each student. The progression from easier to more difficult allows each student initial success in working with the material.

Section Three, "Fun with Words," contains **100 word riddles** and **word puzzles**. Your students will find them interesting and challenging to work.

Part Two, "The Teacher's Guide," consists of three sections that correspond with the three sections of Part One. There are explanations and objectives for each presented skill, answers, and a student self-evaluation progress report that can be duplicated. This is another aspect of THE HANDBOOK that will be a time-saver for you. It will help you with record keeping and also to key the material into management systems if they are in use at your school. It will also allow you to have students check their own answers.

D.R.

Contents

Part Two TEACHER'S GUIDE 273

PART ONE

EXERCISE MATERIAL AND ACTIVITIES FOR YOUR STUDENTS

section one

Selected Reading/Thinking Skills

Skill 1: Finding the Main Idea of a Paragraph or the Central Idea of a Story

Introduction and Examples*

Although there is no foolproof method for finding the main idea, there is a widely used method that has proved to be helpful. In order to use this you should know that a paragraph is always written about something or someone. The something or someone is the topic of the paragraph. The writer is interested in telling his or her readers something about the topic of the paragraph. To find the main idea of a paragraph, you must determine what the topic of the paragraph is and what the author is trying to say about the topic that is special or unique. Once you have found these two things, you should have the main idea. This method is useful in finding the main idea of various types of paragraphs.

Reread the preceding paragraph and state its main idea.

Main idea: _____

_____

_____

Answer: A method helpful in finding the main idea of a paragraph is described.

Let's do another one, and this time let us analyze what we do. Read the following paragraph. After you read the paragraph, choose the word or words that *best* answer the two questions that follow the paragraph.

In high school and in college, John's one goal was athletic success so that he could be in the Olympics. John's goal to be in the Olympics became such an obsession for him that he could not do anything that did not directly or indirectly relate to achieving this goal. He practiced for hours everyday. He exercised, ate well, and had at least eight hours of sleep every night. Throughout school, John allowed nothing and no one to deter him from his goal.

*Adapted from Dorothy Rubin, *Reading and Learning Power* (New York: Macmillan, 1980).

a. What is the topic of the first paragraph?
   1. exercise and practice
   2. work
   3. Olympics
   4. John's goal
   5. athletic success
   6. attempts

Answer: 4

b. What is the author saying about John's goal to be in the Olympics (the topic) that is special and that helps tie the details together?
   1. That John needed time and patience.
   2. That the goal was a good one.
   3. That John needed exercise.
   4. That the goal was not a reasonable one.
   5. That the goal was the most important thing in John's life.
   6. That the goal was an obsession.
   7. That the goal was too much for John.

Answer: 5

If you put the two answers together, you should have the main idea of the paragraph. Main idea: The goal, being in the Olympics, was the most important thing in John's life.

Exercises 8, 9, and 10 are concerned with finding the central idea of a story. We generally use the term *central idea* rather than *main idea* when we refer to a *group* of paragraphs, a story, or an article. The procedure, however, for finding the main idea and for finding the central idea is the same for both.

Skill 1: Finding the Main Idea of a Paragraph

Exercise 1

Directions: *Read the paragraph carefully. Write the main idea of the paragraph in the space below. (Remember that to find the main idea of a paragraph, you must first find the topic of the paragraph; then you must find what is special about the topic. Put the two together, and you should have the main idea.)*

There are at least 250 different species of sharks that can be divided into two different groups. The largest and most common, the sharks themselves, form one. They are easily recognized by their cigar-shaped bodies. The other group includes the skates and rays, which have flattened bodies. The rays' front fins have become large rounded wings, and they literally "fly" through the water.

Main idea: _____

_____

_____

Skill 1: Finding the Main Idea of a Paragraph
Exercise 2

Directions: *Read the paragraph carefully. Write the main idea of the paragraph in the space below. (Remember that to find the main idea of a paragraph, you must first find the topic of the paragraph; then you must find what is special about the topic. Put the two together, and you should have the main idea.)*

Perhaps the lions' most fascinating behavior is their habit of hunting cooperatively. After spotting prey, several lions may fan out while moving slowly toward their quarry. They watch each other's movements carefully. If they see one member along the flank circle around behind the prey, they simply hide themselves and wait. They have learned that prey startled by one lioness may rush into the hidden claws of another.

Main idea: _____
_____
_____

Skill 1: Finding the Main Idea of a Paragraph

Exercise 3

Directions: *Read the paragraph carefully. Write the main idea of the paragraph in the space below. (Remember that to find the main idea of a paragraph, you must first find the topic of the paragraph; then you must find what is special about the topic. Put the two together, and you should have the main idea.)*

The Senoi method may help you end your frightening dreams. If you dream about the same nightmare figure again and again, whether it's a tiger, a witch or Count Dracula, tell yourself that you are going to face it and fight it. The best time to do this is just as you fall asleep, but it will also help if you think about it once in a while during the day. You may have to do this many times, but finally you will beat your nightmare. Once that happens, it may come back as a friend to help you in your dreams. You can even try, as the Senois do, to ask your dream friend for a gift.

Main idea: _____

_____

_____

Skill 1: Finding the Main Idea of a Paragraph

Exercise 4

Directions: *Read the paragraph carefully. Write the main idea of the paragraph in the space below. (Remember that to find the main idea of a paragraph, you must first find the topic of the paragraph; then you must find what is special about the topic. Put the two together, and you should have the main idea.)*

In many parts of Africa, the use of traps, poisons, and dogs has virtually exterminated the leopard. In my youth, we thought that the only good leopard was a hide stretched out for drying. But now we are discovering that the leopard played an important part in maintaining nature's balance. Leopards used to kill thousands of baboons every year, and now that the leopards have been largely wiped out baboons are proving to be a major control problem in many parts of the colony. The perfect way to keep them in check is by allowing their natural enemy, the leopard, to destroy them. So leopards are now widely protected and allowed to increase in numbers. Such is the strange way that man works—first he virtually destroys a species and then does everything in his power to restore it.

Main idea: _____

_____

_____

Skill 1: Finding the Main Idea of a Paragraph

Exercise 5

Directions: *Read the paragraph carefully. Write the main idea of the paragraph in the space below. (Remember that to find the main idea of a paragraph, you must first find the topic of the paragraph; then you must find what is special about the topic. Put the two together, and you should have the main idea.)*

Aunt Polly became concerned about Tom. She began to try all manner of remedies on him. She was one of those people who are infatuated with patent medicines and all newfangled cures. She was an enthusiastic experimenter in those things. When something fresh in this line came out, she was in a fever, right away, to try it; not on herself, for she was never ailing, but on anybody else that came handy. All the "rot" about ventilation and how to go to bed, and how to get up, and what to eat, and what to drink, and how much exercise to take, and what sort of clothing to wear, that was gospel* to her. She never noticed that her health magazines for one month upset everything they had recommended the month before. She was as simple-hearted and honest as the day was long, and so she was an easy victim. She went about to the suffering neighbors, never suspecting that she was not an angel of healing.

Main idea: _____

_____

_____

gospel: from the Bible, meaning "absolutely true" or "not to be doubted."

Skill 1: Finding the Main Idea of a Paragraph

Exercise 6

Directions: *Read the paragraph carefully. Write the main idea of the paragraph in the space below.*

What makes an airplane fly is not its engine nor its propeller. Nor is it, as many people think, some mysterious knack of the pilot, nor some ingenious gadget inside. What makes an airplane fly is simply its shape. This may sound absurd, but gliders do fly without engines, and model airplanes do fly without pilots. As for the insides of an airplane, they are disappointing, for they are mostly hollow. No, what keeps an airplane up is its shape—the impact of the air on its shape. Whittle that shape out of wood, or cast it out of iron, or fashion it, for that matter, out of chocolate and throw the thing into the air. It will behave like an airplane. It will *be* an airplane.

Main idea: _____

_____

_____

Skill 1: Finding the Main Idea of a Paragraph

Exercise 7

Directions: *Read the short paragraph carefully. Try to state its main idea. Read each of the statements, and circle the one that you think best fits your main idea statement. Then explain why you made your choice.*

In our society, food is often associated with recreation. We go out for a snack; invite friends over for a snack; and celebrate special occasions with cakes or big meals. We can't think of baseball without thinking of hot dogs; we can't think of movies without thinking of popcorn; and eating is so often an accompaniment to watching TV that we talk of TV snacks and TV dinners. Just as Pavlov's dogs learned to salivate at the sound of a bell, the activities we associate with food can become signals to eat. Watching TV becomes a signal for potato chips; talking with friends becomes a signal for milk and cookies; nodding over a book tells us it's time for pie and milk.

1. Watching TV signals a need for food.
2. All persons connect food with recreation.
3. Eating is a social activity.
4. Recreation, in our society, often serves as a signal for food.
5. In all societies food is often connected with recreation.

Your main idea: _____
_____
_____

Answer circled: _____
_____
_____

Explanation for choice: _____
_____
_____

Skill 1: Finding the Central Idea of a Story

Exercise 8

Directions: *Read carefully the following short story to determine the central idea of the story. Finding the central idea of a story is similar to finding the main idea of a paragraph. (To find the central idea of the story, find the topic of the story and what is special about the topic.) After you have found the central idea of the story, choose a title for the story that gives readers an idea of what the story is about.*

As the 17-year-old boy entered the telegraph office in Port Huron, Michigan, a gust of wind slammed the door behind him.

"It's not so cold out tonight," he remarked to the telegraph operator. "The ice on the river will begin to move soon."

"Pretty quiet around here," the operator said. "There hasn't been a sound on the wire for the past hour or more."

The boy removed his overcoat, stomped the snow off his boots, and walked to the telegraph machine. He opened the key and began tapping out a test message to the operator at Sarnia, Canada, a mile across the St. Clair River. But the sounder at his elbow failed to register his signals.

"No wonder it's been so quiet around here," he exclaimed. "The wire is dead!"

Alarmed, the operator hurried to the machine. At that moment a man rushed into the office in great excitement.

"There's been an accident out on the river!" he said. "A boat is being crushed in an ice jam. We've got to get word to Sarnia. The only help can come from there."

"That explains the dead wire," said the boy. "The cable to Sarnia must be broken."

For a moment the three stood there, terrified by helplessness. Suddenly the silence was broken by the piercing whistle of the evening train as it pulled into Port Huron. The boy grabbed his coat and rushed from the room.

Running as fast as he could to the railroad yards, he jumped aboard the locomotive as it came to a stop. Hastily he explained the predicament to the engineer. Then, without further delay, he seized the whistle cord and began jerking it in a curious rhythm of long and short blasts.

Then he waited. Seconds later he repeated the blasts, then again and again. Finally he heard an answering far-off whistle.

He decoded the message aloud: "Rescue . . . ship . . . leaving . . . now . . . for . . . damaged . . . vessel." Then he grinned and turned to the telegraph operator who had followed him to the train.

"Good work, son," the operator said. "Just keep using your head like that and some day the world will be hearing a lot about Thomas Alva Edison!"

Central idea: _____
_____
_____

Title: _____
_____
_____

Skill 1: Finding the Central Idea of a Story

Exercise 9

Directions: *Read carefully the following short story to determine the central idea of the story. Finding the central idea of a story is similar to finding the main idea of a paragraph. (To find the central idea of the story, find the topic of the story and what is special about the topic.) After you have found the central idea of the story, choose a title for the story that gives readers an idea of what the story is about.*

A man and his son went to the market one morning. They took along a donkey to bring back whatever they would buy.

As they walked down the road, they met a woman who looked at them with a sour face.

"Are you not ashamed," she called to the father, "to let your little boy walk in the hot sun, when he should be riding on the donkey?"

The father stopped and lifted his boy to the donkey's back. So they went on.

After a little while they met an old man. He began at once to scold the boy. "You ungrateful son!" he shouted. "You let your poor old father walk while you sit there on the donkey like a lazy good-for-nothing!"

When the old man had passed, the father took his frightened son from the donkey and got onto the animal himself.

Futher on they met another man who looked at them angrily. "How can you let your child walk in the dusty road?" he asked. "And you sit up there by yourself!"

The father was troubled, but he reached down and lifted his son up where he could sit on the donkey in front of him.

A little later they met a man and his wife, each of them riding a donkey. The husband called out, "You cruel man! How can you let the poor donkey carry such a heavy load? Get off at once! You are big enough and strong enough to carry the little animal instead of making it carry two of you."

The poor man was now really perplexed. He got off the donkey and took his son off, too.

Then he cut down a young tree for a pole and trimmed it. He tied the donkey's four feet to the pole. Then he and his son lifted the pole. They trudged along, carrying the donkey between them.

As they were crossing a bridge over a stream, they met with a crowd of young men. Seeing the donkey being carried on a pole, they started to laugh and shout. Their noise startled the poor donkey who started to kick violently and broke the ropes holding his feet. As he frisked about, he tumbled off the bridge and was drowned.

The man looked sadly into the stream and shook his head.

"My son," he said to the boy, "you cannot please everybody."

Central idea: _____

_____

_____

Title: _____

_____

_____

Skill 1: Finding the Central Idea of a Story

Exercise 10

Directions: *Read carefully the following short story to determine the central idea of the story. Finding the central idea of a story is similiar to finding the main idea of a paragraph. (To find the central idea of the story, find the topic of the story and what is special about the topic.) Note that in this tale there are actually two topics. State the two topics, and then state the central idea for each. After you have done this, try to write a central idea that would relate to both topics. Then choose a title for the story that best fits your central idea statement.*

Once upon a time the king of a large and rich country gathered together his army to take a faraway little country.

The king and his soldiers marched all morning long and then went into camp in the forest.

When they fed the horses they gave them some peas to eat. One of the Monkeys living in the forest saw the peas and jumped down to get some of them. He filled his mouth and hands with them, and up into the tree he went again, and sat down to eat the peas.

As he sat there eating the peas, one pea fell from his hand to the ground. At once the greedy Monkey dropped all the peas he had in his hands, and ran down to hunt for the lost pea. But he could not find that one pea. He climbed up into his tree again, and sat still looking very glum. "To get more, I threw away what I had," he said to himself.

The king had watched the Monkey, and he said to himself: "I will not be like this foolish Monkey, who lost much to gain a little. I will go back to my own country and enjoy what I now have."

So he and his men marched back home.

Topic: _____

_____

_____

Central idea: _____

_____

_____

Topic: _____

_____

_____

Central idea: _____

_____

_____

Central idea that relates to both topics: _____

_____

_____

Title: _____

_____

_____

Skill 2: Drawing Inferences or "Reading Between the Lines

Introduction and Examples*

Writers count on inference to make their writing more interesting and enjoyable. Rather than directly stating something, they present it indirectly. To understand the writing, the reader must be alert and be able to detect the clues that the author gives. For example, in the sentence *Things are always popping and alive when the twins, Herb and Jack, are around,* you are given some clues to Herb's and Jack's personalities, even though the author has not directly said anything about their personalities. From the statement you could make the inference that the twins are lively and lots of fun to be around.

You must be *careful*, however, that *you do not read more* into some statements than is intended. For example, read the following statements and put a circle around the correct answer. *Example:* Mary got out of bed and looked out of the window. She saw that the ground had some white on it. What season of the year was it? (a) winter; (b) summer; (c) spring; (d) fall; (e) can't tell.

The answer is "(e) can't tell." Many persons choose "(a) winter" for the answer. However, the answer is (e) because the "something white" could be anything; there isn't enough evidence to choose (a). Even if the something white was snow, in some parts of the world, including the United States, it can snow in the spring or fall.

*Dorothy Rubin. *The Vital Arts—Reading and Writing* (New York: Macmillan, 1979).

Skill 2: Drawing Inferences or "Reading Between the Lines

Exercise 1

Directions: *Read carefully each selection. To answer the questions correctly, determine whether enough information is given. Try to answer the questions for each selection without rereading the selection.*

1. As John looked out the train window, he spied leafless trees. What season of the year was it? Circle the correct answer, and give reasons for your answer. (a) winter; (b) summer; (c) spring; (d) fall; (e) can't tell. _____

_____

2. It was a clear bright day, and the sun was directly overhead when we started out on our camping trip. After seven hours of hiking, one-third of our group decided to go back home. The eight of us that were left watched the sun set directly in front of us as we were hiking. It was a beautiful sight.
(a) At what time did the group set out?

Explain: _____

_____

_____

(b) At what time did the sun set?

Explain: _____

_____

_____

(c) How many persons started out on the camping trip?

Explain: _____

_____

_____

(d) In what direction were the campers heading?

Explain: _____

_____

_____

3. Mr. X slithered into the room, casting a chill over all those present. This was his third escape and he was meaner than ever. Who was the man? Circle the correct answer. Explain.

    a. The man was an escaped prisoner.
    b. The man was a policeman.
    c. The man was an inmate in an asylum.
    d. The man was a spy.
    e. You can't tell.

Explain your choice: _____

_____

_____

Skill 2: Drawing Inferences or "Reading Between the Lines"

Exercise 2

Directions: *Read each selection* very carefully. *Without looking back at the selection, try to answer the questions.*

1. The two men looked at each other. They would have to make the decision that might cost many lives. They kept rubbing their hands together to keep warm. Although they were dressed in furs and every part of them was covered except for their faces, they still could feel the cold. The fire that had been made for them from pine trees was subsiding. It was getting light. They had promised their men a decision at dawn. Should they go forward or should they retreat? So many lives had already been lost.

a. Did this take place at the North Pole or South Pole?_____
   How do you know? _____
   _____
   _____

b. Circle the word that best fits the two men. The two men were: (1) trappers (2) officers (3) soldiers (4) guides. Explain why you made your choice.

Explain: _____
_____
_____

c. What inference can you draw from this short passage? Circle the answer.
   (1) The men were on a hunting trip.
   (2) The men were at war with Indians.
   (3) The decision that the two men had to make concerned whether to take an offensive or defensive position in some kind of battle.
   (4) The men were on a hunting trip, but they got caught in a bad storm.

Explain: _____
_____
_____

2. A man builds a house with four sides to it, and it is rectangular in shape. Each side has a southern exposure. A bear comes wandering by. What color is the bear?

Explain: _____

_____

_____

Skill 2: Drawing Inferences or "Reading Between the Lines

Exercise 3

Directions: *Read the following short selection very carefully. Without looking back at the selection, try to answer the questions. Write your answers in the space provided.*

The six remaining children were worn out from walking all day with such heavy knapsacks. They were covered with dust and they were thirsty. They headed toward the mountain range hoping to reach it before the sun finally set behind it. One-third of their companions had decided to turn back one quarter of the way after the trip had started because they had blisters on their feet. The ones who turned back didn't feel that the prize was worth the effort.

1. What kind of day was it?

Explain: _____
_____
_____

2. In what direction were the remaining children heading?

Explain: _____
_____
_____

3. How many children had there been at the beginning of the trip?

Explain: _____
_____
_____

4. Why were the children on this trip?

Explain: _____

_____

_____

5. Were the ones who turned back properly dressed for the journey?

Explain: _____

_____

_____

Skill 2: Drawing Inferences or "Reading Between the Lines

Exercise 4

Directions: *Read carefully the following statements, and answer the questions on each one. Answer the questions in the space provided.*

1. Jane's heart sank when the teacher said, "Pencils down."
   Why did Jane's heart sink when the teacher said, "Pencils down"? ____
   _____

2. The world of sawdust had been good to Hank. He had traveled and met interesting people all over the world.
   What is "the world of sawdust"? _____
   _____

3. Madam Rose, dressed all in red, picked up her battered suitcase and started to walk to the exit. She sighed deeply, hesitated for one brief moment, and then walked on. She knew that she would miss the footlights and everything that went with them.
   What do you think Madam Rose's occupation was? _____
   How do you think Madam Rose feels? _____

4. Jennifer is always surrounded by lots of kids. Whenever you see Jennifer, you can be sure that there will be a crowd.
   What kind of person do you think Jennifer is? _____

Skill 2: Drawing Inferences or "Reading Between the Lines

Exercise 5

Directions: *Read carefully the following statements, and answer the questions on each one. Answer the questions in the space provided.*

1. John and Mary always put a damper on things when they are around. What can you infer about John and Mary from the statement? __
   _____
   _____

2. Pat knew that it would soon be her turn to present her report to the class because her nails were down to the skin of her fingertips.
   How does Pat feel about giving her report? _____
   _____
   _____

3. The man wore a hat, the brim of which seemed to cover his complete forehead; he wore dark sunglasses; the collar of his coat was turned up; and as he walked, he kept throwing quick glances behind his shoulder. What inferences can you make about this man? _____
   _____
   _____

4. Whenever Mrs. Beasley walked into the classroom, all the children stopped chatting and sat at attention.
   Why did the children stop talking when Mrs. Beasley walked into the classroom? _____
   _____
   _____

5. The office staff became confused whenever Mr. Brown gave orders.
   What kind of person do you think Mr. Brown was?_____
   _____
   _____

6. Everyone was always afraid to say anything when Mr. Davis was around.
Why do you think people were afraid to say anything when Mr. Davis was around? _____

_____

_____

7 . Whenever a student was in need of help, he or she went to Mrs. Seale rather than to Mrs. Sloan.
What kind of person do you think Mrs. Seale is? Mrs. Sloan? _____

_____

_____

Skill 2: Drawing Inferences or "Reading Between the Lines

Exercise 6

Directions: *Read the following paragraph carefully. Read each given statement carefully, and then determine whether the statement is "true" or "false." If there is not enough evidence for an answer, write, "can't tell." Write your answer in the space provided.*

Whenever my friend, his brother, and I would walk down the street, we always tried to avoid stepping on the cracks of the sidewalk. No one ever said that we shouldn't, we just didn't. Once my little sister, who likes to follow us, ran in front of us and purposefully stepped on every crack in the sidewalk. Somehow, my friend, his brother, and I felt that our luck changed after that. I know it's peculiar, but we couldn't seem to win one ball game all summer long. What else could it have been but the "cracks"?

_____ 1. The story has three males in it.

_____ 2. The story has at least two males in it.

_____ 3. The person telling the story is a male.

_____ 4. The person telling the story has a younger sister.

_____ 5. Three persons in the story are superstitious.

_____ 6. The persons in the story live in a large city.

_____ 7. The person telling the story, the friend, and his brother played against better players than they.

_____ 8. The game discussed in the story is baseball.

_____ 9. The little girl was fascinated by the cracks in the sidewalk.

Skill 2: Drawing Inferences or "Reading Between the Lines

Exercise 7

Directions: *Read the following paragraph carefully. Read each given statement carefully, and then determine whether the statement is "true" or "false." If there is not enough evidence for an answer, write, "can't tell." Write your answer in the space provided.*

Walking under the blazing sun, which was directly overhead, I felt content and almost joyous. The delicious sun seemed to go right through me. How good it felt! The warmth of the sun always makes me feel good. I wonder if it's because it somehow makes up for the human warmth I crave.

_____ 1. The person is a female.

_____ 2. The person is hitchhiking.

_____ 3. It's summer.

_____ 4. It's about noon.

_____ 5. The person needs affection.

Skill 2: Drawing Inferences or "Reading Between the Lines

Exercise 8

Directions: *Read the following paragraph carefully. Read each given statement carefully, and then determine whether the statement is "true" or "false." If there is not enough evidence for an answer, write, "Can't tell." Write your answer in the space provided.*

I don't know what to do. If I do what they want, I'll get into trouble, and if I don't do what they want, I'll have problems. I knew I was getting in over my head, but I thought that I could handle it. Why is it that some things seem so right at one moment and so wrong at the next? If only I could speak to someone, but I'm afraid to. I know—I'll ask my shadow; however, my shadow will probably say whatever I want it to.

_____ 1. The person speaking in the paragraph is a male.
_____ 2. The story is taking place at night.
_____ 3. The person is in a place with absolutely no light.
_____ 4. The person has a dilemma.
_____ 5. The person is a teen-ager.
_____ 6. The person needs help.
_____ 7. The person is a gambler.

Skill 2: Drawing Inferences or "Reading Between the Lines

Exercise 9

Directions: *Read the following paragraph carefully. Read each given statement carefully, and then determine whether the statement is "true" or "false." If there is not enough evidence for an answer, write, "Can't tell." Write your answer in the space provided.*

"If I can only get through the first day, I'll be fine," thought Terry. "This is my fifth school in four years. We never seem to stay long enough for me to make friends. I wonder what it would be like to be a kid who has a normal home life? Well, I'll probably never know. I better pull myself together and get going. If I'm late I'll be even more conspicuous. Since it's the beginning of the term, I may be able to slip into the classroom and become invisible. I've been able to do that for so long now that I sometimes feel that maybe I am invisible. I always seem to be looking in and watching others. Sometimes I feel like yelling, 'Hey, everybody look at me, look at me; I'm alive! I'm not invisible!' I know I won't do that. Boy, my hands are so cold and my heart is racing so fast—well, here goes. I wish myself luck! Who knows, maybe it'll turn out all right."

_____ 1. The person speaking in the selection is a male.

_____ 2. The person in the selection has gone to a number of schools.

_____ 3. The person in the selection is nervous.

_____ 4. The person's parents are divorced.

_____ 5. The father of the person in the selection is in the army or some branch of the military service.

_____ 6. The person in the selection and his or her family travel a lot.

_____ 7. The person in the selection is timid.

_____ 8. The person in the selection feels that the first day of school is the worst.

_____ 9. The person in the selection has lots of friends.

_____ 10. The person in the selection would like to be noticed.

_____ 11. The person in the selection expects his or her home situation to change.

_____ 12. The person in the selection is somewhat optimistic when he or she enters the classroom.

Skill 2: Drawing Inferences or ''Reading Between the Lines

Exercise 10

Directions: *Read the following paragraph carefully. Read each given statement carefully, and then determine whether the statement is "true" or "false." If there is not enough evidence for an answer, write, "Can't tell." Write your answer in the space provided.*

If I say, "No," they'll think I'm chicken; however, if I go along, I may regret it for the rest of my life. How do I get into these situations? The guys mean well, but they're always just too much for me. I don't want to lose my friends, but I have to live with myself, too. I can just see Dean's face when he finds out. Maybe, I'd better crack the books and take my chances with the guys.

_____ 1. The person is a male.

_____ 2. The person is a high school student.

_____ 3. The person is worried.

_____ 4. The thing that the person is reluctant to do violates the moral or ethical standards of the person.

_____ 5. The thing the person is talking about has to do with playing a prank on Dean.

_____ 6. The person will not go along with the guys.

_____ 7. The person has been in conflict with the guys before.

Skill 3: Categorizing

Introduction and Examples

Categorization is an important skill that you use very often. Every time you put things into groups such as pets, farm animals, wild animals, cities, states, countries, continents, capitals, fruits, vegetables, colors, and so on, you are using the skill of categorizing. When you categorize things, you are classifying things. To be able to classify various things, you must know what things belong together and what things do not belong together. You can classify or categorize things into more general or more specific categories. For example, the category of food is more general than the categories of fruits, vegetables, or nuts; and the category of animals is more general than the categories of pets, wild animals, or tame animals. The category of pets is less general than the category of animals but more general than the categories of dogs or cats. When you outline, you are categorizing.

Examples:

1. Group these words: apple, peach, potato, rice, oats, cucumber, barley peanuts, acorn, pecans, almonds, pear.

Answer:

Nuts	*Fruits*	*Vegetables*	*Grains*
peanuts	apple	potato	rice
acorn	peach	cucumber	oats
pecans	pear		barley
almonds			

2. Circle the word that does not belong.

Airedale   Persian   Angora   Siamese

Answer: *other words refer to cats.*
You should have circled *Airedale* because all the

Skill 3: Categorizing

Exercise 1

Directions: *First read the list of words; then group them in a number of different ways.*

dog	elephant
cat	rhinoceros
chicken	hippopotamus
horse	turkey
cow	duck
tiger	pig
gorilla	

Skill 3: Categorizing

Exercise 2

Directions: *First read the list of words; then group them in a number of different ways.*

Henry Huggins
A History of the United States
"The Johnny Carson Show"
"The Incredible Hulk"
"The Today Show"
"Rockford Files"
"The Jeffersons"
Earthquakes
Earth and the Universe
The Diary of a Young Girl
The Story of My Life

Charlotte's Web
"Laverne and Shirley"
The Study of the Earth
"The Merv Griffin Show"
Little Women
"All in the Family"
Cloth
Why the Earth Quakes
Julie of the Wolves
The Life of George Washington
Young Man in the White House

Skill 3: Categorizing

Exercise 3

Directions: *First find what the items in a group have in common, and then choose a word or phrase from the list below that* best *describes the group. There are more words and phrases than are needed. Put the correct word or phrase on the line after each group of words.*

Words and Phrases: plants, flowers, grains, male animals, animals, females, famous women, fruit, dried fruit, meat, persons, homes, Indian homes, coins, metal, wild animals, animals, tame animals, famous people, famous men, nuts, transportation, states, Northeastern states, Western states, parts of a bird, meat, fowl, books, parts of a horse, presidents, men, parts of a fish, actresses, athletes, vegetables

1. biography, autobiography, novel _____.
2. Betsy Ross, Joan of Arc, Amelia Earhart _____.
3. tiger, bear, cow _____.
4. ferry, bike, train _____.
5. California, Pennsylvania, Alabama _____.
6. Maine, New Jersey, New Hampshire _____.
7. scales, gills, fins _____.
8. hoofs, sides, mane _____.
9. beak, feathers, wings _____.
10. raisin, prune _____.
11. lettuce, celery, carrot _____.
12. drake, rooster, ram _____.
13. tepee, wigwam, igloo _____.
14. George Washington, Abraham Lincoln, John Kennedy _____

   _____.
15. acorns, almonds, pecans _____.
16. oats, barley, rice _____.
17. grass, tree, weed _____.
18. nickel, quarter, can _____.

Skill 3: Categorizing

Exercise 4

Directions: *First find what the items in a group have in common, and then choose a word or phrase from the list below that* best *describes the group. There are more words and phrases than are needed. Put the word or phrase on the line after each group of words.*

Words and Phrases: books, fiction books, nonfiction books, fruit, vegetables, food, cooked food, desserts, dairy products, long books, writing, fowl, animals, tame animals, female animals, wood, wood products, meat, beef, pork, lamb

1. pears, apples, bananas _____
2. meat, tomatoes, apples _____
3. milk, cheese, butter _____
4. jello, applesauce, ice cream _____
5. liver, pork chops, lamb chops _____
6. hen, mare, doe _____
7. biography, autobiography, novel _____
8. biography, autobiography, dictionary _____
9. novel, comics, fairytales _____
10. paper, telephone pole, furniture _____

Skill 3: Categorizing

Exercise 5

Directions: *First read the words in each set to see what they have in common; then circle the word in each set that does not belong. You may use the dictionary to look up unfamiliar words.*

1. Washington, New Hampshire, California, Oregon
2. beetle, bee, wasp, spider
3. clams, oysters, trout, squid
4. husky, schnauzer, porcupine, beagle
5. shark, whale, porpoise, dolphin
6. cloves, cinnamon, nuts, pepper
7. think, understand, ponder, muse
8. stubborn, obstinate, weary, headstrong
9. adder, rattler, cobra, snail
10. money, matter, means, capital

Skill 3: Categorizing

Exercise 6

Directions: *First read the words in each set to see what they have in common; then circle the word in each set that does not belong. You may use the dictionary to look up unfamiliar words.*

1. Indiana, Connecticut, Seattle, Maine
2. large, huge, immense, heavy
3. trumpet, bell, bray, chirp
4. devil, warlock, wizard, witch
5. occult, mysterious, weary, secret
6. dachshund, Siamese, poodle, Schnauzer
7. spiders, ticks, flies, scorpions
8. frogs, snakes, turtles, lizards
9. Albany, Harrisburg, San Francisco, Nashville
10. stove, coal, oil, wood

Skill 3: Categorizing

Exercise 7

Directions: *First read the words in each set to see what they have in common; then circle the word in each set that does not belong. You may use the dictionary to look up unfamiliar words.*

1. barley, oats, pecan, rice
2. buck, bull, sire, dam
3. damsel, dame, maiden, lass
4. hutch, lair, burrow, hut
5. milk, cheese, margarine, butter
6. rose, tulip, lily, hyacinth
7. teacher, instructor, capitalist, professor
8. hangar, terminal, station, garage
9. saw, ax, chisel, drill
10. liver, kidney, brain, rib

Skill 3: Categorizing

Exercise 8

Directions: *First read the words in each set to see what they have in common; then circle the word in each set that does not belong. You may use the dictionary to look up unfamiliar words.*

1. happy, joyous, serious, gay
2. bacon, ham, lamb, pork
3. apples, tomatoes, pears, peas
4. ram, rooster, mare, steer
5. cub, kitten, hen, puppy
6. doe, ewe, hen, sire
7. sides, hooves, dust, mane
8. site, location, house, lot
9. rattler, asp, cobra, snail
10. slender, sturdy, slight, frail
11. clear, lucid, understandable, ambiguous
12. hideous, indolent, repulsive, odious

Skill 3: Categorizing

Exercise 9

Directions: *First read the words in each set to see what they have in common; then circle the word in each set that does not belong. You may use the dictionary to look up unfamiliar words.*

1. scales, fins, wings, gills
2. hippopotamus, giraffe, elephant, rhinoceros
3. Pekingese, Angora, beagle, husky
4. box, hamper, chest, closet
5. biology, anthropology, astrology, astronomy
6. wolf, cougar, jaguar, lion
7. boar, mare, sire, drake
8. fez, cap, beret, cowl
9. tractor, sledge, crane, derrick
10. frigate, ship, liner, raft

Skill 3: Categorizing

Exercise 10

Directions: *First read the words in each set to see what they have in common; then circle the word in each set that does not belong. You may use the dictionary to look up unfamiliar words.*

1. doe, sow, ewe, drake
2. Asia, Europe, India, Africa
3. grape, prune, apricot, pear
4. asp, boa, cobra, wasp
5. jackels, foxes, wolves, cougars
6. duet, quartet, sextant, octet
7. proverb, adage, anecdote, maxim
8. spiders, scorpions, beetles, mites
9. frigate, corvette, yacht, destroyer
10. clarinet, trombone, flute, oboe

Skill 3: Categorizing

Exercise 11

Directions: *First read the words in each set to see what they have in common; then circle the word in each set that does not belong. You may use the dictionary to look up unfamiliar words.*

1. links, court, field, derby, rink
2. house, dwelling, bunk, domicile, quarters
3. chair, table, couch, recliner, rocker
4. Volkswagen, Valiant, Mustang, Bonneville, Aspen
5. table, counter, stand, dais, bar
6. Maine, New Hampshire, Connecticut, Massachusetts, New Jersey
7. want, crave, desire, save, wish
8. point, key, island, bay, ocean
9. toad, salamander, frog, crocodile
10. obstinate, stubborn, sure, dogged, tenacious

Skill 3: Categorizing

Exercise 12

Directions: *First read the words in each set to see what they have in common; then circle the word in each set that does not belong. You may use the dictionary to look up unfamiliar words.*

1. scheme, design, symbol, plan
2. hopeful, gregarious, optimistic, cheerful
3. inborn, innate, inbred, intense
4. indolent, industrious, listless, apathetic
5. thwart, delete, withstand, oppose
6. thrifty, economical, spendthrift, frugal
7. obliterate, erase, raze, decimate
8. terse, infinitesimal, brief, concise
9. belief, doctrine, dogma, problem
10. confident, insecure, assured, optimistic
11. headstrong, tenacious, obstinate, obsessed
12. sage, sophomoric, sensible, wise

Skill 3: Categorizing

Exercise 13

Directions: *First read the words in each set to see what they have in common; then choose the word from the word list that belongs to that set. (Not all words fit in.) Put the word on the line. You may use the dictionary to look up unfamiliar words.*

Word List: squids, sharks, fleas, ticks, butterflies, turtles, larva, million, decameter, kilometer, decimeter, decade, salamanders, asps, seal

1. egg, _____, pupa, adult
2. one, _____, century, millenium
3. meter, _____, centimeter, millimeter
4. scorpions, _____, mites, spiders
5. louse, _____, bee, termite
6. snakes, _____, lizards, crocodiles
7. frogs, _____, toads, newts
8. adders, _____, cobras, rattlers
9. clams, _____, snails, oysters
10. whale, _____, porpoise, walrus

Skill 3: Categorizing

Exercise 14

Directions: *Read each incomplete statement carefully, and then choose a word from the word list that completes the statement and that makes the statement* always *true. A word may be used only once. Put the word in the space provided. You may use the dictionary to look up unfamiliar words.*

Word List: insects, tails, hour, month, minute, second, day, week, year, circle, triangle, persons, chickens, cats, week, kangaroos, liquids, lemons, piglets, child, apples, peas, bean, candy, adult, fish, Siamese, collies, pears, plants

1. Every _____ has twenty-four hours.
2. Every _____ is round.
3. Every _____ has sixty seconds.
4. All _____ are dogs.
5. All _____ are babies.
6. No _____ is round.
7. Most _____ have roots.
8. All _____ are fluids.
9. Female _____ carry their babies in their pouches.
10. No _____ has eight days.
11. All _____ have feathers.
12. Every _____ has at least twenty-eight days.
13. No _____ are vegetables.
14. Some _____ can fly.
15. All _____ are sour.

Skill 3: Categorizing

Exercise 15

> Directions: *Read each incomplete statement carefully, and then choose a word from the word list that completes the statement and makes the statement* always *true. A word may be used only once. Put the word in the space provided. You may use the dictionary to look up unfamiliar words.*

Word List: animals, box, moisture, cherry, ten, five, twenty, human beings, oval, onion, tomato, solids, pound, quart, gallon, half-pound, ounce, fluids, herbivorous, carnivorous, air, sun, moon, snakes

1. A pound of ice weighs the same as a(n) _____ of water.
2. No _____ have limbs.
3. No _____ is a fruit.
4. Many _____ are quadrupeds.
5. Every millennium has _____ centuries.
6. All _____ are bipeds.
7. All horses are _____.
8. All planets have a(n) _____.
9. All gases are _____.
10. Hygrometers measure _____ in the air.

Skill 4: Completing Analogies

Introduction and Examples*

Analogies have to do with relationships. They are relationships between words or ideas. In order to make the best use of analogies or to supply the missing term in an analogy proportion, you must know not only the *meanings* of the words, but also the relationship of the words or ideas to one another. For example, "*doctor* is to *hospital* as *minister* is to ____." Yes, the answer is *church*. The relationship has to do with specialized persons and the places with which they are associated. Let's try another one: *beautiful* is to *pretty* as ____ is to *decimate*." Although you know the meanings of *beautiful* and *pretty* and you can figure out that beautiful is more than pretty, you will not be able to arrive at the correct word to complete the analogy if you do not know the meaning of *decimate*. *Decimate* means "to reduce by one tenth" or "to destroy a considerable part of." Because the word that completes the analogy must express the relationship of more or greater than, the answer could be *eradicate* or *annihilate,* because these words mean "to destroy completely."

Some of the relationships that words may have to one another are similar meanings, opposite meanings, classification, going from particular to general, going from general to particular, degree of intensity, specialized labels, characteristics, cause-effect, effect-cause, function, whole-part, ratio, and many more. The preceding relationships do not have to be memorized. You will gain clues to these from the pairs making up the analogies; that is, the words express the relationship. For example: "*pretty* is to *beautiful*"—the relationship is degree of intensity: "*hot* is to *cold*"—the relationship is one of opposites; "*car* is to *vehicle*"—the relationship is classification.

*Dorothy Rubin. *Gaining Word Power* (New York: Macmillan, 1978).

Skill 4: Completing Analogies

Exercise 1

Directions: *Find the relationship between a pair of words, and then complete each analogy with the* best *word from the word list. There are more words given in the word list than you need. The first is done for you. You may use the dictionary to look up unfamiliar words.*

Word List: hen, male, female, big, bother, assist, water, face, spice, warm, hot, cold, hospital, nurse, ram, animal, drake, fowl, deer, nickel, quarter, self, dollar, another, book, fig, fruit, dessert, grape, meat, solid, food, bandage, mouth, low

1. Up is to down as high is to _____ low _____.
2. Minister is to church as doctor is to _____.
3. Pretty is to beautiful as cool is to _____.
4. Juice is to liquid as beef is to _____.
5. Mare is to horse as doe is to _____.
6. Chicken is to rooster as duck is to _____.
7. Cent is to dime as dime is to _____.
8. Prune is to plum as raisin is to _____.
9. Car is to vehicle as pepper is to _____.
10. Frighten is to scare as annoy is to _____.
11. Torn is to ripped as aid is to _____.
12. Biography is to another as autobiography is to

    _____.

13. Wrist is to arm as nose is to _____.

Skill 4: Completing Analogies

Exercise 2

Directions: *Find the relationship between a pair of words, and then complete each analogy with the best word from the word list. There are more words given in the word list than you need. The first is done for you. You may use the dictionary to look up unfamiliar words.*

Word List: sick, well, singe, coal, mare, win, lioness, best, least, better, hundred, ten, thousand, warn, hurt, shout, save, cub, baby, wear, tornado, clothing, robin, plume, eyes, scale, more, most, much, tail, heavy, short

1. Young is to old as tall is to _____short_____.
2. Chicken is to hen as horse is to _____.
3. Fat is to heavy as healthy is to _____.
4. Chicken is to feather as fish is to _____.
5. Hammer is to tool as coat is to _____.
6. Furnace is to heat as compete is to _____.
7. Hot is to warm as burn is to _____.
8. Dog is to puppy as lion is to _____.
9. Train is to transport as alarm is to _____.
10. Good is to best as less is to _____.
11. Tap is to strike as whisper is to _____.
12. Millimeter is to centimeter as one is to _____.

Skill 4: Completing Analogies

Exercise 3

> **Directions:** *Find the relationship between a pair of words, and then complete each analogy with the* best *word from the word list. There are more words given in the word list than you need. The first is done for you. You may use the dictionary to look up unfamiliar words.*

Word List: bank, clothes, banking, client, solo, patient, joy, judge, last, second, horse, colt, wizard, sow, homonym, chase, car, transmission, weak, antonym, lost, found, cold, warm, freeze, adept, unskilled, wetter, dry, job, play, tired, quartet

1. Stop is to go as first is to _____last_____.
2. Ram is to drake as mare is to _____.
3. Princess is to prince as witch is to _____.
4. Slow is to fast as synonym is to _____.
5. Two is to duet as four is to _____.
6. Help is to aid as hunt is to _____.
7. Like is to love as chill is to _____.
8. Bough is to tree as clutch is to _____.
9. Hotel is to guest as hospital is to _____.
10. Rip is to tear as skilled is to _____.
11. Condensation is to wet as evaporation is to

    _____.

12. Hobby is to boating as vocation is to _____.

Skill 4: Completing Analogies

Exercise 4

Directions: *Find the relationship between a pair of words, and then complete each analogy with the* best *word from the word list. There are more words given in the word list than you need. The first is done for you. You may use the dictionary to look up unfamiliar words.*

Word List: sun, moon, light, cold, kilometer, pour, year, rate, ship, day, compass, torrent, cards, blizzard, doe, time, era, kind, drove, dame, ram, century, place, ewe, love, cub, binary, meter, ecstasy, chirp, moo, friend, hate, millimeter

1. Happy is to sad as night is to _____ day _____ .
2. Dog is to bark as bird is to _____ .
3. Good is to best as rain is to _____ .
4. See is to saw as drive is to _____ .
5. Horse is to mare as deer is to _____ .
6. One is to ten as decade is to _____ .
7. Chicken is to rooster as sheep is to _____ .
8. Drizzle is to downpour as like is to _____ .
9. Sad is to miserable as joy is to _____ .
10. Ten is to decimal as two is to _____ .
11. One is to thousand as meter is to _____ .
12. Centimeter is to millimeter as decameter is to

_____ .

13. Hint is to disclose as drip is to _____ .
14. Card is to deck as deck is to _____ .
15. Distance is to odometer as direction is to

_____ .

Skill 4: Completing Analogies

Exercise 5

Directions: *Find the relationship between a pair of words, and then complete each analogy with the* best *word from the word list. There are more words given in the word list than you need. The first is done for you. You may use the dictionary to look up unfamiliar words.*

Word List: sudden, toe, cyclone, body, arrest, child, baby, guilty, girl, mouth, charge, boy, strike, kid, always, pet, immediately, never, touch, breeze, storm, vegetable, better, least, salad, house, less, acquit, kitten, much, Persian, winter, fall, spike, hundred, century, bicentennial, tepee, worst, raisin, fruit

1. Plum is to prune as grape is to_____raisin_____.
2. Apple is to fruit as cabbage is to _____.
3. Good is to bad as best is to _____.
4. Eskimo is to igloo as Indian is to _____.
5. Finger is to nail as face is to _____.
6. Sheep is to lamb as goat is to _____.
7. More is to less as most is to _____.
8. Dog is to collie as cat is to _____.
9. Rain is to hurricane as wind is to _____.
10. Ten is to decade as hundred is to _____.
11. Tepid is to hot as pat is to _____.
12. One is to two as centennial is to _____.
13. Splendid is to spectacular as tack is to _____.
14. Vain is to conceited as abrupt is to _____.
15. Haughty is to arrogant as indict is to _____.

Skill 4: Completing Analogies

Exercise 6

Directions: *Find the relationship between a pair of words, and then complete each analogy with the* best *word from the word list. There are more words given in the word list than you need. The first is done for you. You may use the dictionary to look up unfamiliar words.*

Word List: clothing, powerful, dress, fearful, enemy, clean, cent, quarter, dollar, sewing, frozen, ice, melt, help, fruit, apricot, frigid, solid, water, prune, equal, seam, adequate, perfect, transport, capture, warn, carry, absorb

1. Juice is to liquid as beef is to _____solid_____.
2. Warm is to hot as cold is to _____.
3. Penny is to dime as dime is to _____.
4. Handle is to pot as stitch is to _____.
5. Grape is to raisin as plum is to _____.
6. Mountain is to hill as superior to _____.
7. Teeth is to bite as alarm is to _____.
8. Shovel is to dig as towel is to _____.
9. Costume is to disguise as truck is to _____.
10. Equivalent is to equal as potent is to _____.

Skill 4: Completing Analogies

Exercise 7

Directions: *Find the relationship between a pair of words, and then complete each analogy with the* best *word from the word list. There are more words given in the word list than you need. The first is done for you. You may use the dictionary to look up unfamiliar words.*

Word List: pearl, some, flower, patient, hospital, carry, most, much, whack, less, ten, money, years, grass, disclose, century, plant, command, belt, help, harm

1. Apple is to fruit as rose is to _____flower_____.
2. Always is to never as more is to _____.
3. Minister is to church as doctor is to _____.
4. Dime is to dollar as decade is to _____.
5. Fox is to animal as weed is to _____.
6. Deck is to ship as buckle is to _____.
7. Damp is to soaked as hint is to _____.
8. Terrible is to dire as belt is to _____.
9. Saw is to cut as litter is to _____.
10. Fat is to plump as suggest is to _____.

Skill 4: Completing Analogies

Exercise 8

Directions: *Find the relationship between a pair of words, and then complete each analogy with the* best *word from the word list. There are more words given in the word list than you need. You may use the dictionary to look up unfamiliar words.*

Word List: ignorant, arrogant, remorseful, state, establish, deny, dress, coat, scarf, quartet, fire, preface, dialogue, wizard, destroy, epilogue, hollow, pomposity, increase, boulder, stone, cliff, dog, cat, lizard, turtle

1. Solo is to duet as duet is to _____.
2. Lass is to lad as witch is to _____.
3. Beginning is to prologue as ending is to _____.
4. Gnu is to antelope as iguana is to _____.
5. Most is to least as affirm is to _____.
6. Hill is to mountain as pebble is to _____.
7. Instrument is to microscope as accessory is to

   _____.

8. Modest is to humble as proud is to _____.
9. Ambulance is to transport as dynamite is to

   _____.

10. Depression is to dejection as inflation is to

    _____.

Skill 4: Completing Analogies

Exercise 9

Directions: *Find the relationship between a pair of words, and then complete each analogy with the* best *word from the word list. There are more words given in the word list than you need. You may use the dictionary to look up unfamiliar words.*

Word List: slow, helpful, posthaste, attitude, tornado, breeze, blow, instrument, small, huge, organ, abyss, extemporaneous, prepared, grain, eat, destroy, explosive

1. Snow is to blizzard as wind is to _____.
2. Position is to post as immense is to _____.
3. Stove is to cook as dynamite is to _____.
4. Rain is to drop as sand is to _____.
5. Coal is to fuel as spade is to _____.
6. Foresight is to hindsight as impromptu is to

   _____.
7. Lazy is to indolent as speedy is to _____.
8. Pepper is to spice as liver is to _____.
9. Impudent is to insolent as posture is to _____.
10. More is to most as pit is to _____.

Skill 4: Completing Analogies

Exercise 10

Directions: *Find the relationship between a pair of words, and then complete each analogy with the* best *word from the word list. There are more words given in the word list than you need. You may use the dictionary to look up unfamiliar words.*

Word List: vegetarian, doctor, veterinarian, ewe, small, ram, mammoth, malign, astronomer, ornithologist, ichthyologist, interest, stag, save, want, help, cub, pup, millennium, century, million, tadpole, command, hint, drone, adder

1. Insect is to bee as snake is to _____.
2. Goat is to kid as seal is to _____.
3. Child is to pediatrician as animal is to _____.
4. Simmer is to boil as suggest is to _____.
5. Chicken is to rooster as deer is to _____.
6. Haughty is to arrogant as huge is to _____.
7. Rock is to geologist as bird is to _____.
8. Optimist is to pessimist as defend is to _____.
9. Alarm is to warn as bank is to _____.
10. One is to thousand as thousand is to _____.

Skill 4: Completing Analogies

Exercise 11

Directions: *Find the relationship between a pair of words, and then complete each analogy with the* best *word from the word list. There are more words given in the word list than you need. You may use the dictionary to look up unfamiliar words.*

Word List: tired, wilted, taut, temper, shock, elevator, shriek, trumpet, direction, pile, straw, birds, plants, flowers, naive, petal, insects, pistil, animals, scorpions, termites, beeltes, bees, million, one, hundred, compact, ecstatic

1. Sad is to miserable as happy is to _____.
2. Hundred is to ten as thousand is to _____.
3. Six is to flies as eight is to _____.
4. Male is to stamen as female is to _____.
5. Wet is to dry as limp is to _____.
6. Bird is to chirp as elephant is to _____.
7. Attitude is to posture as agreement is to _____.
8. Ichthyologist is to fishes as entomologist is to

    _____.
9. Hay is to bale as grain is to _____.
10. Fictitious is to real as sophisticated is to _____.

Skill 4: Completing Analogies

Exercise 12

Directions: *Find the relationship between a pair of words, and then complete each analogy with the* best *word from the word list. There are more words given in the word list than you need. You may use the dictionary to look up unfamiliar words.*

Word List: pen, pay, hold, rake, lark, knife, quiver, fold, falcon, roe, owl, stable, enough, animal, render, dove, hole, less, more, hoe, stub

1. Swine is to sty as sheep is to _____.
2. Room is to house as stall is to _____.
3. Panther is to leopard as hawk is to _____.
4. Chew is to masticate as melt is to _____.
5. Gun is to holster as arrow is to _____.
6. Spoon is to shovel as fork is to _____.
7. Stall is to delay as stump is to _____.
8. Wine is to grape as caviar is to _____.
9. Mind is to obey as remuneration is to _____.
10. Early is to prompt as extra is to _____.

Skill 4: Completing Analogies

Exercise 13

Directions: *Find the relationship between a pair of words, and then complete each analogy with the* best *word from the word list. There are more words given in the word list than you need. You may use the dictionary to look up unfamiliar words.*

Word List: obstinate, more, most, artist, doctor, lawyer, example, antenna, less, pacify, dash, moccasin, pole, arctic, signal, arouse, cry, help

1. Minor is to major as least is to _____.
2. Believable is to credible as stubborn is to _____.
3. Office is to doctor as studio is to _____.
4. Head is to beret as foot is to _____.
5. Bullhorn is to amplify as beacon is to _____.
6. South is to antarctic as north is to _____.
7. Dormant is to inactive as calm is to _____.
8. Bond is to bind as bolt is to _____.
9. Deer is to antler as insect is to _____.
10. Modern is to recent as model is to _____.

Name ____ Class ____ Date ____

Skill 4: Completing Analogies

Exercise 14

Directions: *Find the relationship between a pair of words, and then complete each analogy with the* best *word from the word list. There are more words given in the word list than you need. You may use the dictionary to look up unfamiliar words.*

Word List: declare, barren, aid, prologue, state, epilogue, vehicle, avocation, deny, vacation, crypt, secret, final, foremost, latter, arrest, millennium, century, year

1. Error is to mistake as assist is to _____.
2. Entrance is to exit as admit is to _____.
3. Beginning is to end as former is to _____.
4. Ten is to decade as hundred is to _____.
5. Hamper is to hinder as hobby is to _____.
6. Letter is to postscript as book is to _____.
7. Siren is to warn as anchor is to _____.
8. Proud is to humble as lush is to _____.
9. Hamper is to container as vault is to _____.
10. Pine is to tree as train is to _____.

67

Skill 4: Completing Analogies

Exercise 15

Directions: *Find the relationship between a pair of words, and then complete each analogy with the* best *word from the word list. There are more words given in the word list than you need. You may use the dictionary to look up unfamiliar words.*

Word List: physician, specialist, pediatrician, duplicate, biweekly, monthly, spectacular, pedestrian, spectacle, annual, spectator, weekly, automaton, fold, bring, bifocals, unite, plant, stars, sailing, underwater, friendly

1. Brutal is to savage as viewer is to _____.
2. Hear is to racket as view is to _____.
3. Riding is to walking as motorist is to _____.
4. Scientist is to chemist as doctor is to _____.
5. Solo is to duet as weekly is to _____.
6. Automobile is to vehicle as robot is to _____.
7. Astronaut is to space as aquanaut is to _____.
8. Hate is to detest as join is to _____.
9. Autograph is to signature as copy is to _____.
10. Stale is to fresh as hostile is to _____.

Skill 5: Following Directions

Introduction and Example

Being able to follow directions is an important skill that you use all your life. Scarcely a day goes by without the need to obey directions. Cooking, baking, taking medication, driving, traveling, repairing, building, planning, taking examinations, doing assignments, filling out applications, and a hundred other common activities require the ability to follow directions.

You can learn to be better at following directions through practice and by heeding the pointers given below.

1. Read the directions *carefully*. Do *not* skim directions. Do not take anything for granted and, therefore, skip reading a part of the directions.
2. If you do not understand any directions, do not hesitate to ask your teacher and/or another student.
3. Concentrate! People who follow directions well have the ability to concentrate well.
4. Follow the directions that *are* given, not the ones that you think ought to be given.
5. Reread directions if you need to, and refer to them as you follow them.
6. Remember that some directions should be followed step by step.
7. Practice following directions. Try this activity, which will give you experience in following directions.

> **Directions:** *Read carefully the entire list of directions that follows before doing anything. You have four minutes to complete this activity.*

1. Put your name in the upper right-hand corner of this paper.
2. Put your address under your name.
3. Put your telephone number in the upper left-hand corner of this paper.
4. Add 9370 and 5641.
5. Subtract 453 from 671.
6. Raise your hand and say, "I'm the first."
7. Draw two squares, one triangle, and three circles.
8. Write the opposite of *hot*.
9. Stand up and stamp your feet.
10. Give three meanings for *spring*.

11. Write the numbers from one to ten backward.
12. Write the even numbers from two to twenty.
13. Write the odd numbers from one to twenty-one.
14. Write seven words that rhyme with *fat*.
15. Call out, "I have followed directions."
16. If you have read the directions carefully, you should have done nothing until now. Do only directions 1 and 2.

Answer: The directions stated that you should read the entire list of directions carefully *before doing anything*. You should have done only directions 1 and 2. When you take timed tests, you usually do *not* read the directions as carefully as you should.

Name _____ **Class** _____ **Date** _____

Skill 5: Following Directions

Exercise 1

Directions: *Read each numbered instruction carefully, and then carry it out on the boxed material.*

INSTRUCTIONS

1. If the number of circles is equivalent to the number of squares and tri-angles, put a dot in the last circle.
2. If the number of triangles preceding the four letters is equal to the number of circles in the box, put a cross on the third letter in the box.
3. If there are three consecutive* figures—each one different from the others—in the box, circle the third consecutive figure.
4. If the number of letters is equal to the number of digits in the box and if both letters and digits follow one another, put a dot in the first square.
5. If two consecutive digits added together equal the third digit, put a dot in the second square.

Consecutive means "following one after another."

Skill 5: Following Directions

Exercise 2

Directions: *Read each numbered instruction carefully, and then carry it out on the boxed material.*

```
                              C  D  E  G  I  99  75  85
40 50 45 set get log pat R S T U V W X 9 8 7 4 6 5
over  large  under
```

INSTRUCTIONS

1. If the number of letters is equal to the number of numbers and there are more than nine of each, put a cross on the first letter.
2. If there are three numbers one after the other, that have a sum that is less than 19 and more than 16, circle the three numbers.
3. If there is a word that is the opposite of *under* and a word that rhymes with another word that causes a mist, as well as two other rhyming words, underline these words.
4. If there are seven letters in order, a word the opposite of *small,* three numbers that added together equal 17, and two other numbers that added together equal 17, put a cross on the three numbers and circle the two other numbers.
5. If the number of letters is more than the number of words but equal to the number of numbers and if there are fewer double-digit numbers than single-digit numbers, circle the word that rhymes with *mat.*
6. If the number of letters in order is an odd one, if the single-digit numbers added together equal less than any of the two-digit numbers, and if there are more than three numbers that have five in them, circle all the numbers with five and underline the middle letter of the alphabet in order.

Skill 5: Following Directions

Exercise 3

Directions: *Read each numbered instruction carefully, and then carry it out on the given circles.*

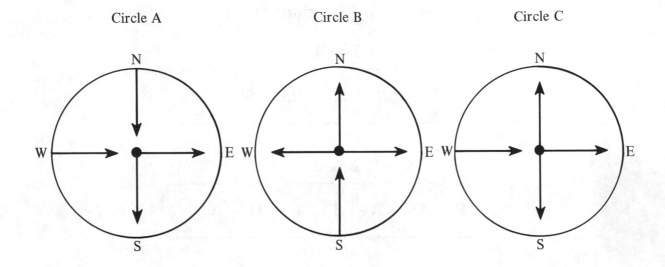

Circle A   Circle B   Circle C

INSTRUCTIONS

1. If not all three circles have an arrow pointing N, put a circle around the W in the first circle.
2. If any of the arrows in either circle B or circle C are not pointing S, put a circle around E in circle C.
3. If the arrows in circles A and B together are pointing in every direction put a circle around N in circle B.
4. If the arrows in circle B and the arrows in circle C are pointing in every direction in each circle, put a circle around S in circle C.
5. If arrows in circles A, B, and C, are pointing W and N in each circle, put a circle around W in circle C.

Skill 5: Following Directions

Exercise 4

Directions: *Read each numbered instruction carefully, and then carry it out on the Following Directions Sheet.*

Following Directions Sheet

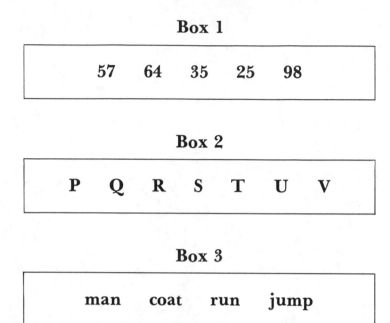

Box 1

| 57 | 64 | 35 | 25 | 98 |

Box 2

P Q R S T U V

Box 3

man coat run jump

INSTRUCTIONS

1. In box 1 circle the number that is equal to (6 × 6) minus 1, and in box 3 circle the second letter of the third word.

2. Circle the middle letter in box 2, the first letter of the fourth word in box 3, and the number equal to (5 × 5) in box 1.

3. Put a cross on the letter before *S* in box 3, a circle around the number equal to (10 × 10) minus 2 in box 1, and a circle around the second vowel in the second word in box 3.

4. Put a circle around the last consonant in the last word in box 3, and a cross on the number in the fifties in box 1.

5. Put a circle around the letter after *U* and a cross on the letter before *Q* in box 2; put a circle around the first word in box 3 and a cross on the last letter of the second word; put a cross on the number equal to (8 × 8) in box 1.

Skill 5: Following Directions

Exercise 5

Directions: *Read each numbered instruction once only, and then carry out the instructions on the boxed material. (This activity requires a great amount of concentration.)*

> 1 7 3 4 play dog man M N O P Q 35 32 63 15
> 10 stop under big

INSTRUCTIONS

1. If there are two numbers that added together equal 7 and a word that rhymes with *may*, put a line under the rhyming word.
2. If there is a word that means the same as *large*, a word opposite to *go*, and a word that rhymes with *fan*, put a circle around the three words.
3. If there are two numbers that added together equal 8, two numbers that added together equal 67, and a word the opposite of *over*, underline the two numbers that added together equal 8.
4. If there are five consecutive letters, four words that each contain a different vowel, and at least four odd numbers, put a cross on the five consecutive letters.
5. If there are six words, three even numbers, two numbers that added together equal 45, and three numbers that added together equal 16, do nothing.
6. If there are two numbers that added together equal 25, two numbers that added together equal 95, and three numbers that added together equal 79, put a circle around the three numbers that added together equal 79.

Skill 5: Following Directions

Exercise 6

Directions: *Read each numbered instruction* once *only, and then carry out the instructions on the boxed material. (This activity requires a great amount of concentration).*

```
coat   30   76   54   23   red   A   B   C   D   E
green  yellow  7  6  5  4  3  2  1  P  Q  R  T  V
in   short   nice   IX   X   XI
```

INSTRUCTIONS

1. If there is a word opposite to *tall* and a word that rhymes with *boat,* put a line over the two words.
2. If there is a color that signals cars to stop, to go, and to slow down, put a line over the color that signals cars to slow down.
3. If there are four odd numbers in order and three even numbers in order, put a line under the largest odd number in order.
4. If there are three numbers one after the other that added together equal 12 and if there are two numbers added together one after the other that equal less than 12, put a line over the three numbers that added together equal 12.
5. If there are four numbers one after the other that equal 20 and a word that rhymes with *slice,* put a circle around the rhyming word.
6. If there are two vowels, if there are five letters in order, if there are five odd numbers, and if there are two single-digit numbers that, multiplied together, equal a two-digit number, circle the two-digit number and the two single-digit numbers.
7. If three consecutive numbers added together equal 6, if four consecutive numbers added together equal 18, and if there are two Roman numerals that added together equal 19, put a line under the Roman numeral X.

Skill 5: Following Directions

Exercise 7

Directions: *Read each numbered instruction once only, and then carry out the instructions on the boxed material. (This activity requires a great deal of concentration.)*

```
1.  *  *  *  A  B  C  D  E
2.  R  S  T  U  V  fill
3.  boat  76  15  9  12  1  3  7  goat
4.  over  run  fan  7  9
5.  *  *  N  O  P  Q  fun  under
```

INSTRUCTIONS

1. If there are two words that are in the same line that rhyme and two words that are not in the same line that rhyme, put a line under the two rhyming words that are in different lines.
2. If there are 14 letters, five stars, and eight words, put a check over the middle letter in line 2.
3. If two numbers added together and three numbers added together equal 16 in line 3 and two numbers added together equal 16 in line 4, underline the two numbers in line 4.
4. Put a cross on the word that rhymes with *fun*, a circle around the opposite of *under*, and a line over the word that rhymes with *will*.
5. Put a line under the second star in line 1, a line over the fourth number in line 3, and a cross on the largest number in line 3.
6. Put a circle around the first letter in line 1, a cross on the third letter in line 2, and a check over the second word in line 4.
7. Put a check over the third star in line 1, a circle around each of the two numbers that appear in the same line and added together equal 24, a line under the word that rhymes with *can*, and a circle around the third, fifth, and seventeenth letters of the alphabet.

Skill 5: Following Directions

Exercise 8

Directions: *Read each numbered instruction* once *only,*
and then carry it out on the given circles.

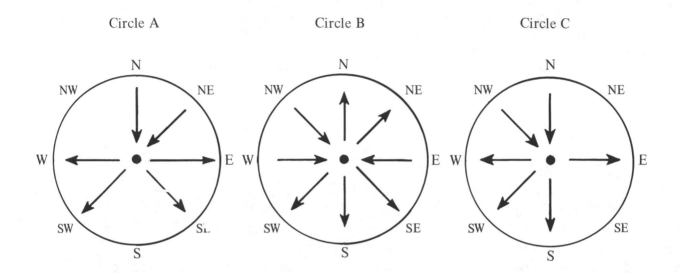

Circle A   Circle B   Circle C

INSTRUCTIONS

1. If arrows in each of the three circles are pointing N, NE, S, and SE,
   put a circle around S in circle B.
2. If arrows in each of the circles B and C are pointing W, S, and SW,
   put a circle around SW in circle A.
3. If the arrows in circle C are pointing in the same directions as all the
   arrows in circle A, put a circle around S in circle A.
4. If arrows in each of the three circles are pointing in three directions
   that are similar in each of the three circles, put a circle around N in
   circle C.
5. If the arrows in circles A, B, and C are missing at least one direction in
   each circle, put a circle around NW in circle B.

Skill 5: Following Directions

Exercise 9

Directions: *Read each numbered instruction once only, and then carry out the instructions on the boxed material.*

Following Directions Sheet

Box 1

○   ○   ○   □   □

Box 2

| 12 | 24 | 100 | 72 | 15 |

Box 3

| rope | can | red | gone |

Box 4

| L | M | N | O | P | Q |

INSTRUCTIONS

1. Put a dot in the middle figure in box 1, a cross on the number that is 1 less than (5 × 5) in box 2, and a circle around the second letter of the first word in box 3.

2. Put a cross on the first square in box 1, a dot in the second circle in box 1, a circle around the second vowel in the fourth word in box 3, and a cross on the number equal to (10 × 10) in box 2.

3. In box 3, put a circle around the first letter of the fourth word, a cross on the third letter of the third word, a circle around the second letter of the third word, and a cross on the third letter of the first word.

4. In box 2, circle the number that is equal to 1 less than (4 × 4); in box 4, circle the letter before *N*, and the letter after *O*, in box 3, circle the third letter of the second word.

5. Put a cross on the first letter of the third word and the second vowel in the first word in box 3; put a cross on the third letter in box 4; put a circle around the last square in box 1; put a circle around the number equal to (4 × 3) in box 2.

Skill 5: Following Directions

Exercise 10

Directions: *Read each numbered instruction* once *only,* *and then carry out the instructions in the boxed material.* *(This activity requires a great deal of concentration).*

7	9	4	6	but		give		late
get	D	E	F	G	H	10		let

INSTRUCTIONS

1. If there are the same number of numbers as letters and two numbers added together equal another number, circle the two numbers.
2. If there are two words that rhyme and four different vowels in all of the words, put a circle around the third letter of the second word.
3. If there are the same number of words, letters, and numbers and if two numbers multiplied together equal 24, circle the second vowel of the third word.
4. If three numbers added together equal 23 and two numbers added together equal 13, circle the middle letter of the alphabet letters, the third letter of the fifth word, and a word that rhymes with *hut*.
5. If there are three even numbers, five words, and three numbers that added together equal 26, put a cross on the three numbers that equal 26, on the words that have two vowels, and on a word that rhymes with *hut*.

Skill 6: Finding Inconsistencies

Introduction and Example

Good readers are alert readers. You should not believe everything you read. If something does not make sense, you should question it even if it is a textbook written by an authority in the field. For example, if in your science book you found the statement "Humans drink about 1,000 quarts of fluid in a week," would you believe it? Reread it. Does it make sense? Of course not. Think about it. Why doesn't it make sense? Answer: There are only seven days in a week. Even if someone drank four quarts of fluid a day (which is a large amount), that person would still have had only 28 quarts of fluid. The "1,000" is an obvious error. The author probably meant to say ten quarts.

Sample: Underline the word in the following sentence that does not make sense.

The dictator was very democratic and harsh.

Answer: You should have underlined *democratic*. The author probably meant to use the word "autocratic."

Skill 6: Finding Inconsistencies

Exercise 1

Directions: *Read each sentence carefully. Find the word in each sentence that does not make sense, and replace it with one from the word list that does make sense in the sentence. Not all words fit in. Words may be used only once.*

Word List: space, plane, meat, vegetables, pleased, hay, rising, nights, straw, wild, low, season, heavy, sun, foods, moon, milk, safe, fur, thick, dried, Noah, men, days, Job, silver

1. At daybreak you could see that the sun was slowly setting.

   _____

2. In Africa we hunted such tame game as lions, elephants, and hippopotamuses. _____

3. We were told not to walk or skate on the frozen lake because the ice was too thin to be dangerous. _____

4. The stars in the sky twinkle brilliantly most dawns.

   _____

5. The farmer laid the eggs in the box to make a comfortable bed for the newborn puppies. _____

6. I love to eat such fools as ice cream, cake, fruit, and salad.

   _____

7. Two animals from every species were taken aboard the ark by Moses.

   _____

8. The captain radioed the ground controls that his ship was in trouble.

   _____

9. We love to pet the soft feathers of our dog. _____

10. My brother gave me five shiny gold dollars as a birthday present.

   _____

11. The spices we used to sweeten the meat were salt, pepper, and paprika. _____

12. The displeased employer nodded in agreement as his star employee gave an excellent talk. _____

Skill 6: Finding Inconsistencies

Exercise 4

> **Directions:** *Read the paragraph* carefully. *Underline the word that does not make sense. Choose a word from the word list that replaces the inconsistency.*

Word List: rain, rainy, home, work, week, morning, one, sun, setting, windy, day, once, three-fourths, two-fifths, leaving, east, west, north, south, starved, satiated, eastern, western, southern, northern, sunny, one-third

It is noon, and the moon is directly overhead. There isn't a cloud in the sky. It is a clear, overcast day. Everyone agrees that it is a perfect night for the school's annual picnic. Twice a year the Deerville School, which is located in the northern section of Deerville, holds a picnic for its students. Usually, three-fifths of the students attend whereas about two-thirds don't. The picnic is held in the southern side of town right on school grounds. There is so much to eat and so much to do that everyone is generally fatigued and famished by sunset. At that time, it is customary to sing the school song while watching the rising sun. Shortly after, most depart for school. Students living in the eastern part of town head toward the sun, whereas people living in the western part of town head away from the sun.

1. _____
2. _____
3. _____
4. _____
5. _____
6. _____

7. _____
8. _____
9. _____
10. _____
11. _____

Skill 6: Finding Inconsistencies

Exercise 5

Directions: *Read the paragraph carefully. Underline the word or phrase that does not make sense. Explain why it does not make sense.*

The American commander, John Jefferson, an alien in the United States, is in the U.S. Air Force. He was chosen to fly the scientists in the new jet because he was an accomplished equestrian. His plane was to take a group of disinterested scientists on a special trip for which they had planned all year. They were going to study the tombs of the Pharaohs along the banks of the Amazon. These noted astrologists had learned about some watches that had been found near the tombs. They were supposed to be thousands of years old, but the scientists were unimpressed by the news. Jefferson told the scientists that the journey would start in the United States and that they would head toward the North Pole.

1. _____   6. _____
2. _____   7. _____
3. _____   8. _____
4. _____   9. _____
5. _____

Skill 7: Distinguishing Between Fact and Opinion

Introduction and Examples

It is important to determine whether information you read is factual or not. Often opinions are presented as though they are facts. *Opinions are not facts.* Opinions are expressions of attitudes or feelings about something. Opinions can vary from person to person; they cannot be conclusively proved right or wrong. Facts, on the other hand, do not change from person to person. Facts can be proved true.

Examples of opinions: Science fiction films are good. China would be an interesting place to visit. Arithmetic is hard.

Examples of facts: Washington, D.C., is the capital of the United State. A kilometer equals 1,000 meters. There are four quarts in a gallon.

Sample: In front of each sentence put the letter *F* if it's a fact or the letter *O* if it's an opinion.

_____ 1. Sharon is a good tennis player.

_____ 2. Oxygen is a colorless, odorless, and tasteless gas necessary for life.

Answers: 2. F

1. O

Skill 7: Distinguishing Between Fact and Opinion

Exercise 1

Directions: *Read each sentence carefully. Determine whether the sentence is expressing a fact or an opinion. In front of each sentence put the letter F if it's a fact or the letter O if it's an opinion. (Remember that facts do not change from person to person as opinions do.)*

_____ 1. I like to play ball.

_____ 2. It's fun to play ball.

_____ 3. My sister is pretty.

_____ 4. Arithmetic is hard.

_____ 5. The sun is a star.

_____ 6. It's important to know how to drive.

_____ 7. Certain vaccinations help prevent disease.

_____ 8. Life without any homework would be good.

_____ 9. Hamburgers and hot dogs are delicious.

_____ 10. Mrs. Robinson's class won the baseball tournament.

Skill 7: Distinguishing Between Fact and Opinion

Exercise 2

Directions: *Read each sentence carefully. Determine whether the sentence is expressing a fact or an opinion. In front of each sentence put the letter F if it's a fact or the letter O if it's an opinion. (Remember that facts do not change from person to person as opinions do.)*

_____ 1. Tatum O'Neal, the actress, is pretty.

_____ 2. David Cassidy is a good singer.

_____ 3. The Beatles are great singers.

_____ 4. Biology is a science.

_____ 5. Everyone should study biology.

_____ 6. Alligators live along the edges of large bodies of water.

_____ 7. Cake is better than bread.

_____ 8. Playing football is more tiring than playing basketball.

_____ 9. A fact is always a true statement.

_____ 10. A bathroom in the house is more important that a television set.

Skill 7: Distinguishing Between Fact and Opinion

Exercise 3

Directions: *Read each sentence carefully. Determine whether the sentence is expressing a fact or an opinion. In front of each sentence put the letter F if it's a fact or the letter O if it's an opinion. (Remember that facts do not change from person to person as opinions do.)*

_____ 1. Fanning yourself is a good way to keep cool.

_____ 2. Farm life is hard.

_____ 3. The pioneers were courageous.

_____ 4. Salt is necessary for life.

_____ 5. Energy can be converted into different forms of energy.

_____ 6. Bob Hope is the best of all the comedians.

_____ 7. Inflation causes the dollar to be worth less.

_____ 8. Swimming is a better sport than boating.

_____ 9. It's more difficult to breathe in high altitudes than in low altitudes.

_____ 10. A comic book is not as good as a regular storybook.

Skill 7: Distinguishing Between Fact and Opinion

Exercise 4

Directions: *Read each sentence* carefully. *Determine whether the sentence is expressing a fact or an opinion. In front of each sentence put the letter* **F** *if it's a fact or the letter* **O** *if it's an opinion. (Remember that facts do not change from person to person as opinions do.)*

_____ 1. A citrus fruit has more Vitamin C than a chocolate.

_____ 2. Reading is better than watching television.

_____ 3. An opinion is what someone believes or the way someone feels.

_____ 4. Fat people are all cheerful.

_____ 5. History tells us about past events.

_____ 6. A hippopotamus has very thick skin.

_____ 7. Soda is better than water.

_____ 8. Not all birds can fly.

_____ 9. The museum is a good place to visit.

_____ 10. You can depend on his word.

Skill 7: Distinguishing Between Fact and Opinion

Exercise 5

Directions: *Read each sentence* carefully. *Determine whether the sentence is expressing a fact or an opinion. In front of each sentence put the letter* F *if it's a fact or the letter* O *if it's an opinion. (Remember that facts do not change from person to person as opinions do.)*

_____ 1. Water is necessary to life.

_____ 2. Man is an animal.

_____ 3. A weed is a plant.

_____ 4. A spider is not technically an insect.

_____ 5. A fish makes a good pet.

_____ 6. *Sire* refers to the male parent of four-footed animals.

_____ 7. Computers can think.

_____ 8. A tomato is a fruit.

_____ 9. A whale is a mammal.

_____ 10. Friends are trustworthy.

_____ 11. Bears are dormant during the winter.

_____ 12. Snakes are vicious animals.

Skill 8: Detecting Propaganda Techniques and Bias

Introduction and Examples

People use propaganda techniques and bias to win us over to their way of thinking. Propaganda helps to further one's own cause or damage someone else's cause. Propaganda techniques and bias bend the truth and often make it hard for us to distinguish between what is fact and what is not.

Propaganda is defined as the act of causing one to be impressed and eventually filled with some view. The term *propaganda* is associated with deception or distortion. In other words, people who use propaganda are trying to influence persons by using deceptive methods.

Bias refers to *a mental leaning, a partiality, a prejudice,* or *a slanting of something*.

From the two definitions, you can see that persons interested in propagandizing something have a certain bias. They use propaganda techniques to distort information to indoctrinate people with their own views or bias.

Some Propaganda Techniques

Type of Propaganda	Examples
1. Name calling—denouncing a person by tagging him with a widely condemned label	Cheapskate, chisler, Red, and so on
2. Glittering generalities—seeking acceptance of ideas by associating them with words widely accepted and approved	Freedom, businesslike, American, Christian, democratic, and so on
3. Transfer—citing respected sources of authority, prestige, or reverence in such a way as to make it appear they approve the proposal	The home, the Constitution, will of the people, public education, the church, the flag, and so on
4. Testimonial—using testimonials from famous people to build confidence in a product	For TV commercials—actors, athletes, personalities, and so on, support a certain product
5. Card stacking—building on half-truths	Through careful selection of favorable evidence and an equally careful ommision of unfavorable or contrary evidence
6. Plain folks—seeking some favor through establishing someone as "just one of the boys"	Presidential candidates photographed in Indian war bonnets or politicians shown milking cows, and so on
7. Bandwagon—going along; because everybody is doing some certain thing, you ought to do it too	A commercial saying: "The majority of people eat Crunchies. Are you one of these?"

Skill 8: Detecting Propaganda Techniques

Exercise 1

Directions: *Read each of the following sentences carefully. Each sentence uses a propaganda technique. After reading each sentence, determine what propaganda technique is being used. Put your answer in the space provided.*

1. If Major Blimp is for it, you know it's good.

   _____

2. Why be different? Use Krazzel! _____

3. Only radicals would talk that way. _____

4. If you're businesslike, you'll do it. _____

5. Jack Jones, a star athlete, uses Brand X shaving cream, so it must be good. _____

6. Let's not listen to him because he's probably a swindler.

   _____

7. Be in. Wear Product Z. _____

8. In the course of freedom, we must come out against that.

   _____

9. If John Jones, the noted singer, drives an ERX car, you know it's special. _____

10. Let's vote for him; he is so American. _____

Skill 8: Detecting Propaganda Techniques

Exercise 2

Directions: Read each of the following sentences carefully. Each sentence uses a propaganda technique. After reading each sentence, determine what propaganda technique is being used. Put your answer in the space provided.

1. Don't be the last kid on your block to get Frizzles.
   _____

2. Chocos are good for you. Eat them with a glass of milk, and you'll get all the nourishment you need for breakfast. _____

3. David Cassidy, a well-known actor says, "I've been driving an FBA car for some time, and I'm happy with it. I wouldn't drive any other car." _____

4. A political candidate says to a group of people, "Folks, it's good to be here with you. There's nothing I enjoy better than visiting with you hardworking people. I know what it's like because I've worked hard all my life just like you." _____

5. Be in. Wear Jeano's jeans. _____

6. I wouldn't listen to a stooge like him. _____

7. She's so democratic. _____

8. The Constitution states that everyone has a right to protect himself or herself. Join our club. We believe in self-protection, too.
   _____

9. This is a fantastic deal! For only a few cents down and a dollar a month, you can own this Brazzle. _____

10. Only troublemakers would talk that way. _____

Skill 8: Detecting Propaganda Techniques

Exercise 3

Directions: *Read the following selection carefully. Underline the phrases in the selection that are examples of propaganda. State the propaganda technique used for each of your underlined phrases.*

Fortunately, the school election will be over soon. I don't think that I can stand another week such as the last one. First there was John, who told me that I was the only one not voting for his candidate "True-Blue Tim." Then there was Mary, who told me that if I were a student with lots of school spirit, I'd be out campaigning for her candidate, "Fathead Jane." Mary says that the majority of students are supporting her candidate. She says that even the famous local star thinks that Jane is the best person. Personally, I think that both their candidates are creeps, and I don't intend to vote for either one. I'm going to vote for Jennifer because she is so democratic and fair.

1. _____
2. _____
3. _____
4. _____
5. _____
6. _____
7. _____
8. _____

Skill 8: Detecting Bias

Exercise 4

Directions: *Read each statement* carefully. *Determine the author's purpose in each one. Write* positive *if the author wishes you to feel* positively *and* negative *if the author wishes you to feel* negatively.

1. What a glaring color that is! _____
2. What a striking color that is! _____
3. That was a gourmet feast. _____
4. That was a vulgar display of food. _____
5. How obscene to waste so much food. _____
6. The hostess outdid herself. _____
7. The film struck out. _____
8. The only redeeming feature in the film was its scenery.

   _____
9. The film is a masterpiece. _____
10. What a nosy person he is! _____
11. Her speeches are always confusing. _____
12. Her speeches are always double-talk. _____
13. Her speeches always give both sides of the issue.

    _____
14. That is a white elephant. _____
15. Isn't Jim too familiar? _____

Skill 8: Detecting Bias

Exercise 5

Directions: *Read each headline* carefully. *State whether the writer is neutral (has no favorites), has a favorite (state the favorite), or is negative. Make one choice only for each headline.*

1. a. Jefferson's Team No Match for Jackson's Team
   _____

   b. Jefferson's Team Has Off Night — Loses to Jackson's Team
   _____

   c. Jefferson Team to Play Jackson Team Tonight
   _____

   d. Jackson's Team Is Slaughtered _____

   e. Jefferson Team Plays Poorly _____

   f. Jefferson's Team Goes Down Valiantly Against Jackson's Team
   _____

2. a. Sims to Play Harrison _____
   b. Harrison Cinch to Beat Sims _____
   c. Sims Outmatched Against Harrison _____
   d. Match Rated Toss-up _____
   e. Sims More Performer Than Player _____
   f. Harrison Serious Contender for the Title _____

Skill 9: Using Divergent Thinking to Solve Problems

Introduction and Examples

Divergent thinking requires that you go beyond the obvious to solve a problem. Good divergent thinkers look for alternate ways to solve problems. They recognize that there are usually many ways to solve problems, not just one set way. Good divergent thinkers can usually come up with many different ways to use an object.

Example: State the many different uses of a brick.

Answers:

And so on . . .

A brick can be used as a paper weight.

A brick can be carved out and used as an ashtray.

A brick can be used to write with.

A brick can be used as a bedwarmer.

A brick can be used as a weapon.

A brick can be used to build a wall.

If you stated only uses that included building, you were not being very divergent. To be divergent, you had to go beyond the obvious uses of a brick.

Skill 9: Using Divergent Thinking to Solve Problems

Exercise 1

Directions: *Read each problem carefully. Solve each of the problems by looking beyond the obvious.*

1. If you went to bed at eight o'clock at night and set your analog alarm clock to get up at nine o'clock in the morning, how many hours of sleep would this permit you to have?. _____

2. Why can't a man living in Winston-Salem, North Carolina, be buried west of the Mississippi River? _____

3. An archaeologist claimed that he found some gold coins dated 46 B.C. Do you think he did? Explain. _____

4. Is it legal in North Carolina for a man to marry his widow's sister?

   _____

5. A woman gives a beggar 50 cents. The woman is the beggar's sister, but the beggar is not the woman's brother. How is this possible?

   _____

6. A farmer had 17 sheep. All but nine died. How many did he have left? _____

7. Divide 30 by one-half and add 10. What is the answer?

   _____

Skill 9: Using Divergent Thinking to Solve Problems

Exercise 2

Directions: *Read each problem* carefully. *Solve each of the problems by looking beyond the obvious.*

1. Think of the Roman numeral nine. Subtract three from the Roman numeral nine. By adding one symbol to the Roman numeral nine, you should have the correct answer. What is it? _____

2. Do they have a Fourth of July in England?
   _____

3. How many birthdays does the average man have?
   _____

4. Some months have 30 days; some have 31. How many have 28 days? _____

5. The first part of an odd number is removed, and it becomes even. What number is it? _____

Skill 9: Using Divergent Thinking to Solve Problems

Exercise 3

Directions: *Read each problem* carefully. *Solve each of the problems by looking beyond the obvious.*

1. Take 2 apples from 3 apples and what do you have? _____

2. I have in my hand two United States coins that total 55 cents in value. One is not a nickel. Please bear that in mind. What are the two coins? _____

3. If you had only one match and entered a room in which there were a kerosene lamp, an oil heater, and a woodburning stove, which one would you light first? _____

4. If a doctor gave you three pills and told you to take one every half-hour, how long would they last you? _____

5. In the following line drawing, how many squares are there? _____

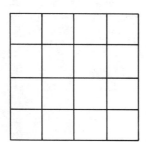

Skill 9: Using Divergent Thinking to Solve Problems

Exercise 4

Directions: *Read each problem carefully. Answer the question at the end of each problem. To solve each problem, you must look beyond the obvious.*

1. A father and his little girl were crossing a street when suddenly a car swerved and hit the little girl. The frantic father stopped a passing car and had the driver rush them to the hospital. At the hospital the child was prepared for surgery. The surgeon arrived, looked at the child, and said, "Oh, no! She's my daughter." How can this be? _____

_____

2. Two football teams were playing a championship game. Five touchdowns were made, but not one man made a touchdown. How is this possible? _____

_____

3. Two nurses were chatting with a doctor. Another doctor came by and said, "Say, is this strictly a stag party?" Why did the other doctor ask the question? _____

_____

4. While a group of engineers were discussing a design problem, their supervisor entered and asked, "Hey, haven't you guys solved the problem yet? We've held up the meeting long enough. We have to begin." A short while after the meeting began, the supervisor had to be rushed to the hospital. The next day one of the engineers called to find out how the supervisor was doing. The supervisor replied, "I'm doing fine, but the baby is in an incubator." Can you explain this? _____

_____

_____

Skill 9: Using Divergent Thinking to Solve Problems

Exercise 5

Directions: *Read each problem carefully. Solve each of the problems by looking beyond the obvious.*

1. Here is a dot matrix. It consists of nine dots. You have to connect the dots with four straight lines, going through each dot only once and without lifting your pencil from the paper.

```
•   •   •

•   •   •

•   •   •
```

2. Read the following short selection, and solve the mystery.

Three murderers killed their victim in a sauna. They left the sauna without the weapon. The police came and found no trace of the weapon. How was the victim killed, and what was the weapon used?

3. Following are some words. See if you can determine which words would fit in between *A* and *horrible*? Note that *be* follows *A*.

A be _____ _____ _____ _____ _____ horrible.

section two

Vocabulary Expansion Skills

Skill 10: Using Combining Forms (Word Parts) to Expand Vocabulary*

Introduction and Examples

As a means of helping you to use combining forms to increase your vocabulary, some terms should be defined. There are a great number of words that combine with other words to form new words, for example, *grandfather* (*grand* + *father*) and *policeman* (*police* + *man*)—both compound words. Many root (base) words are combined with a letter or additional letters—either at the beginning (prefix) or at the end (suffix) of the root (base) word—to form a new, related word, for example *replay* (*re* + *play*) and *played* (*play* + *ed*).

In the words *replay* and *played, play* is a root, *re* is a prefix, and *ed* is a suffix. A *root* is the smallest unit of a word that can exist and retain its basic meaning. It cannot be divided further. *Replay* is not a root word because it can be divided into *re* and *play*. *Play* is a root word because it cannot be divided further and still keep a meaning related to the root word.

Combining forms are usually defined as roots borrowed from another language that join together or that join with a prefix, a suffix, or both a prefix and a suffix to form a word. Often the English combining forms are derived from Greek and Latin roots. Because the emphasis in this book is on the building of vocabulary meanings rather than on the naming of word parts, prefixes, suffixes, English roots, and combining forms, will *all* be referred to as combining forms. *Combining forms in this book are defined as any word part that can join with another word or word part to form a word or a new word.*

You will see the power of combining forms when you realize that, by knowing a few combining forms, you can unlock the meanings of many, many words. For example, by knowing the following combining forms, you can define correctly many terms used in the metric system as well as other words.

Examples

deca — ten
deci — tenth
cent, centi — hundred, hundredth
milli — thousand, thousandth
(*Centi, milli,* and *deci* are usually used to designate "part of.")

*Adapted from Dorothy Rubin. *Gaining Word Power* (New York: Macmillan, 1978.)

decameter — ten meters
decimeter — 1/10 meter
centimeter — 1/100 meter
millimeter — 1/1000 meter
decade — period of ten years
century — period of one hundred years
centennial — one hundredth year anniversary
millennium — period of 1,000 years

Skill 10: Using Combining Forms to Expand Vocabulary

Exercise 1

Directions: *A. Look carefully at the words that are made up of each combining form. From the words, try to figure out the meaning of the combining form. B. Match the combining form in column 2 to the meaning in column 1.*

A. 1. bi — bimonthly, biweekly, bicycle _____

2. anni, annu, enni   annual, biannual, biennial, anniversary

_____

3. bio — biology, biography _____

4. ology — geology, anthropology _____

5. cent, centi — century, bicentennial, centennial _____

6. auto — autograph, autobiography _____

7. graph — autograph, biography _____

8. ped, pod — pedestrian, pedal, peds, biped _____

9. dic, dict — dictation, diction, dictator _____

10. spect — spectacle, spectator, inspect _____

B.

	Column 1	Column 2
_____	1. two	a. ology
_____	2. year	b. cent
_____	3. life	c. auto
_____	4. study of	d. dict
_____	5. hundred	e. bio
_____	6. self	f. bi
_____	7. something written	g. graph
_____	8. foot	h. spect
_____	9. say	i. ped
_____	10. see	j. anni

Skill 10: Using Combining Forms to Expand Vocabulary

Exercise 2

Directions: *Study the combining forms and their meanings. Read each sentence carefully. Read the words in the word list. Use your knowledge of the combining forms and their meanings to help you figure out what word best fits each blank in each sentence. Define each word.*

Combining Forms and Meanings: bi = two; cylco = wheel, circle; bio = life; cent = hundred; deca = ten; ology = the study of; chrono = time; ped, pod = foot; ped = child

Word List: bicycle, biology, century, decade, cyclone, chronological, biped, podiatrist, pediatrician

1. I like to ride my _____. _____

2. We are taking _____ in school this year because we want to learn about living things. _____

3. Our teacher asked us to write our outline in _____ order.
   _____

4. Man is a(n) _____ because he walks on two legs.
   _____

5. My mother took my baby sister to a(n) _____ for her check-up. _____

6. We will be entering a new _____ in the year 2000.
   _____

7. When my feet hurt, my mother took me to a(n) _____.
   _____

8. I have lived for more than a(n) _____. _____

9. The _____ was so strong that it destroyed many houses in our town. _____

Skill 10: Using Combining Forms to Expand Vocabulary

Exercise 3

Directions: *Study the combining forms and their meanings. Read each sentence carefully. Read the words in the word list. Use your knowledge of the combining forms and their meanings to help you figure out what word best fits each blank in each sentence. Define each word.*

Combining Forms and Meanings: arch = rule; mono = one; auto = self; a = without; gamy = marriage; bi = two; leg = law; theo = god

Word List: monarchy, anarchy, theocracy, legal, monarch, autocracy, autocrat, mongamy, bigamy, atheist, legislature

1. _____ is not _____ in the United States. _____ ; _____

2. _____ is practiced in the United States.
   _____

3. In a(n) _____ , a king, queen, or emperor is called a(n) _____ . _____ ;
   _____

4. _____ , as a form of government, does not exist today as it did in the Middle Ages and before. _____

5. The persons elected to the _____ should be very dependable and trustworthy. _____

6. In a(n) _____ the _____ has absolute control. _____ ;
   _____

7. A(n) _____ would not be a churchgoer.
   _____

8. In the West years ago, when there were no laws, a state of _____ existed. _____

Skill 10: Using Combining Forms to Expand Vocabulary

Exercise 4

Directions: *Study the combining forms and their meanings. Read the words in the word list. Define them. Read each sentence carefully. Choose the word that* best *fits the blank in each sentence.*

Combining Forms and Meanings: in = not; cred = believe; fin = end; micro = very small; tele = from afar; scope = a tool or instrument used to see; audio = hear

Word List:

finish_____   infinite _____

credible _____   incredible_____

microscope _____   telescope _____

auditorium _____   inaudible _____

audience _____

1. The _____ listened carefully to every word the speaker said.

2. In my biology class we use the _____ to help us to see very small objects.

3. The sailor looked through the _____ to see if he could spot land.

4. Because time goes on and on, it is _____ .

5. My mother said that I had to _____ my homework, before I could go out to play.

6. The story he told about seeing a man as tall as a five-story building was too _____ to believe.

7. The speaker speaker spoke so softly that his voice was
   (a) _____ to everyone in the large
   (b) _____ .

8. His story sounded like a(n) _____ one, and everyone believed him.

Skill 10: Using Combining Forms to Expand Vocabulary

Exercise 5

Directions: *Study the combining forms and their meanings. Read each sentence carefully. Read the words in the word list. Use your knowledge of the combining forms and their meanings to help you figure out what word best fits each blank in each sentence. Define each word.*

Combining Forms and Meanings: ali = other; vis = see; poten = powerful; in, im = not

Word List: alias, alien, alienate, potent, potentate, potential, inalienable, impotent, visible, invisible

1. In the film the _____ man was not able to be seen by anyone. _____

2. On a clear day the skyline of the city is _____.
_____

3. A criminal uses a(n) _____ because he or she doesn't want his or her identity to be known. _____

4. A citizen of another country is a(n) _____ in the United States. _____

5. I try very hard not to _____ anyone because I don't like to have any enemies. _____

6. In the United States each person has certain _____ rights. _____

7. The drug was so _____ that it knocked out the 250-pound man in a matter of seconds. _____

8. We all felt _____ because we could do nothing about the situation. _____

9. The _____ was in complete control of his country, and no one dared oppose him. _____

10. The acorn has the _____ to become an oak tree. _____

Skill 10: Using Combining Forms to Expand Vocabulary

Exercise 6

Directions: *Study the combining forms and their meanings. Read each sentence carefully. Read the words in the word list. Use your knowledge of the combining forms and their meanings to help you figure out what word best fits each blank in each sentence. Define each word.*

Combining Forms and Meanings: *sci, scio = know; poten = powerful; omni = all; co, cor, com, col, con = together; ven, veni = come; ion, sion, tion = act of, state of; pro = before, forward; log, logo = speech, word*

Word List: omnipotent, potent, omniscient, science, omnipresent, convention, convene, convenient, logical, prologue

1. It is not possible for a human being to be _____
   and _____. _____;
   _____

2. She is the most _____ leader we have had, and as
   a result we have gained much from her leadership.

   _____

3. When I am older, I will major in some area of _____
   because I like to observe, study, and experiment.

   _____

4. The argument you presented was so _____ that
   no one had any difficulty following your reasoning.

   _____

5. Every year the teachers go to a(n) _____ to share
   ideas and learn about new things. _____

6. My poetry book has a(n) _____ at the beginning
   of it. _____

7. It is not _____ for me to attend the meeting on a
   Saturday. _____

8. The chairperson said that the meeting would _____
   in about ten minutes. _____

9. The _____ toothpaste commercial was beginning to annoy me because it seemed to be on all the time.
_____

Skill 10: Using Combining Forms to Expand Vocabulary

Exercise 7

Directions: *Study the combining forms and their meanings. Read each sentence carefully. Read the words in the word list. Use your knowledge of the combining forms and their meanings to help you figure out what word best fits each blank in each sentence. Define each word.*

Combining Forms and Meanings: *mob, mot, mov = move; im, in = not; auto = self; pro = before, forward; de = away, from*

Word List: motion, mobile, immobile, motive, automobile, automotive, motor, demoted, promoted, mobilized

1. We live in a(n) _____ home because we like to travel a lot. _____

2. The police said that the suspect had the opportunity and means to commit the crime, but they did not know his _____.
   _____

3. When the _____ in our boat stopped, we were stranded in the middle of the lake. _____

4. My brother's friend was _____ because he was not doing a very good job. _____

5. I have been _____ every year in school.
   _____

6. The _____ of the ship makes me seasick.
   _____

7. The _____ man appeared to be dead.
   _____

8. My father's _____ has power steering.
   _____

9. Any _____ vehicle is self-propelling.
   _____

10. The troops were _____ after the attack.
    _____

Skill 10: Using Combining Forms to Expand Vocabulary

Exercise 8

Directions: *Study the combining forms and their meanings. Read each sentence in Part A carefully. Using the combining forms and their meanings, define each underlined word. In Part B use the combining forms and their meanings to build a word that fits the blank in each sentence.*

Combining Forms	Meanings	Combining Forms	Meanings
a	without	milli	thousand
aqua	water	naut	sail, explore
astro	star	ology	the study of, the science of
auto	self		
bi	two	ped, pod	foot
bio	life	pseudo	false
cent	hundred	sci	know
cyclo	wheel, circle	scope	see, view
deca	ten	tele	from a distance
geo	earth	tox	poison
graph	something written, machine		

Part A

1. Good <u>pedestrians</u> should follow traffic laws when walking across busy streets in the city. _____

2. In 1876 we celebrated our <u>centennial</u> birthday. _____

3. I wonder what the world will be like in the next <u>century</u>. _____

4. A <u>million</u> years ago, life was much different from what it is today. _____

5. I may take a course in <u>geology</u> because I like to learn about the makeup of the earth. _____

6. The chemicals were so <u>toxic</u> that a small dose could kill you. _____

7. <u>Astronomy</u> is another subject I would like to learn more about.

_____

8. <u>Astrology</u> is called a <u>pseudoscience</u> by many.

_____ ; _____

9. Snakes are <u>apodal</u> animals. _____

10. After our long hike, my feet hurt so much that I had to visit a <u>podiatrist</u>. _____

Part B

1. When I am well-known, people will ask for my

_____ .

2. When I am older, I would like to be a(n) _____ and explore underseas.

3. It doesn't seem possible that I have already lived a whole

_____ .

4. Because I love to study fish, my parents bought me a(n)

_____ for my birthday.

5. Perhaps I will become a(n) _____ and visit Mars.

6. We are studying about living things in my

_____ class.

7. I use my _____ to view the distant stars.

8. We celebrated our _____ in the year 1976.

9. When I am older, I may decide to write my own

_____ because others will be interested in knowing about me.

10. One of my favorite subjects in school is _____ because I like to learn about countries and continents.

Skill 10: Using Combining Forms to Expand Vocabulary

Exercise 9

Directions: *Study the combining forms and their meanings. Using the combining forms and their meanings, try to figure out the meanings of the words in the word list. Choose the word from the word list that best fits the blank in each sentence. (Check the dictionary for any word that you are not sure of.)*

Combining Forms and Meanings: *grat = pleasing; in = not; con = with, together; ous = full of, having; jud, judi, judic = judge; pre = before*

Word List: gratuity, ingrate, gratuitous, gratitude, congratulated, gratified, judicious, prejudiced

1. It _____ her to have her friend wear her gift.

2. _____ persons are usually not interested in looking at all the evidence.

3. Everyone _____ him when he made the final point that won the game.

4. The decision was a(n) _____ one, and it was bound to be hailed as a step forward in bettering employer-employee relations.

5. We couldn't believe our ears when we were told that our _____ was not enough.

6. As I am not used to receiving _____ services, I insisted on paying something.

7. The _____ that the parents felt toward the doctor who had saved their child's life could not be put into words.

8. What a(n) _____ he is to behave in such a manner after we did so much for him.

Skill 10: Using Combining Forms to Expand Vocabulary

Exercise 10

Directions: *Study the combining forms and their meanings. Using your knowledge of the combining forms and their meanings, try to figure out the meanings of the words in the word list. Choose the word from the word list that best fits each blank in each sentence. (Check the dictionary for any word that you are not sure of.)*

Combining Forms and Meanings: *pel, puls = drive, push, throw; com = with, together; pro = forward, before, in front of; re = back, again; im = not, in, into; dis = not, take away, deprive of; ex = out, from*

Word List: repellent, repelled, propel, pulse, compel, dispel, expel, impulsive

1. My friend is very rash and _____.
2. The leaders said that they would _____ the dethroned monarch rather than kill him.
3. The engineers decided to design an engine tht would use a different form of energy to _____ airplanes.
4. The insect spray acted more as an attraction than as a(n) _____.
5. The coaches were trying to _____ all rumors about their star athlete.
6. Nobody can _____ me to do something I really do not want to do.
7. We were completely _____ by their uncalled-for behavior.
8. Opinion polls try to gauge the nation's _____

Skill 11: Expanding Vocabulary with Homographs

Introduction and Examples

Because many words have more than one meaning, the meaning of the word is determined by how the word is used in a sentence. You must be careful to use those words with many meanings correctly. In the following pairs of sentences, notice how the same underlined word conveys different meanings:

1. That is a large <u>stack</u> of books.
2. <u>Stack</u> the books here.

1. The <u>train</u> had a lot of passengers.
2. Do you <u>train</u> your own dog?

1. The dogs <u>bark</u> at night in my neighborhood.
2. The <u>bark</u> of the tree is peeling.

From these, you can see that the way the word is used in the sentence will determine its meaning. Words that are spelled the same but have different meanings are called *homographs*. You should be able to grasp the meaning of homographs from the sentence context (the words surrounding a word that can throw light on its meaning). For example, note the many uses of *capital* in the following sentences.

1. That is a <u>capital</u> idea.
2. Remember to begin each sentence with a <u>capital</u> letter.
3. The killing of a policeman is a <u>capital</u> offense in some states.
4. Albany is the <u>capital</u> of New York State.
5. In order to start a business, you need <u>capital</u>.

Each of the preceding sentences illustrates one meaning for *capital*.

In sentence 1 *capital* means "excellent."
In sentence 2 *capital* means "referring to a letter in writing that is an uppercase letter."
In sentence 3 *capital* means "punishable by death."
In sentence 4 *capital* means "the seat of government."
In sentence 5 *capital* means "money or wealth."

Some homographs are spelled the same but do not sound the same. For example, *refuse* means "trash"; *refuse* means "to decline to accept." In sentence 1 in the examples, *refuse* (ref´ use), meaning "trash," is pronounced differently from the term *refuse* (re fuse´) meaning "to decline to accept" in sentence 2. In reading, you can determine the meaning of *refuse* from the way it is used in the sentence (context clues).

Examples of homographs:

1. During the garbage strike there were tons of uncollected *refuse* on the streets of the city.
2. I *refuse* to go along with you in that project because it seems unethical to me.

Do not confuse *homonyms* or *homophones* (words that sound alike but have different spellings and meanings) with homographs.

Examples of homonyms or homophones:

pear, pare; to, two, too; way, weigh; fare, fair; two, tow; plain, plane.

Skill 11: Expanding Vocabulary with Homographs (Words That Are Spelled the Same but Have Different Meanings)

Exercise 1

Directions: *Read each sentence carefully. Think of a word that is spelled the same but has different meanings that would fit all the blanks of the sentence and make sense. Insert the word in the blanks. The first is done for you.*

1. I _____can_____ carry that heavy _____can_____ because I am very strong.

2. My mother does not like me to _____ when she sends me to the store to buy a(n) _____ of bread.

3. I took a sweater out of my _____ and then went to the medicine _____ to take some aspirin for my _____ cold.

4. The _____ told his bride that he would _____ her to be able to _____ horses.

5. The _____ act caused people to revolt to try and _____ it out.

6. When the coal _____, which is _____, was destroyed by a(n) _____, we were unable to _____ it anymore.

7. It's fun to _____ down the _____.

8. From the _____ of her voice, you could tell that it wasn't a(n) _____ idea to go swimming in the _____.

9. If you _____ easily, avoid fixing a flat _____.

10. Because of the _____, the boss has to _____ everyone.

Skill 11: Expanding Vocabulary with Homographs (Words That Are Spelled the Same but Have Different Meanings)

Exercise 2

Directions: *Read each sentence carefully. Think of a word that is spelled the same but has different meanings that would fit all the blanks of the sentence and make sense. Insert the word in the blanks.*

1. In the _____, the leaves _____.

2. It's not _____ that on such a(n) _____ day, I can't go to the _____.

3. Please tell _____ that I need to borrow his _____ to _____ up my car.

4. It is _____ to see that you like _____ rather than showy things.

5. In the _____ I have avoided discussing my _____ because I feel that what is _____ is _____.

6. I find that I _____ better in my _____ at home than in _____ hall at school.

7. He gave the burglar a(n) _____ on the head with his _____.

8. At the track _____we usually _____ many people we know.

9. The _____ is an insect that can _____.

10. Joe, standing by the tree _____, said that none of my questions could _____ him.

Skill 11: Expanding Vocabulary with Homographs (Words That Are Spelled the Same but Have Different Meanings)

Exercise 3

Directions: *Read each sentence carefully. Think of a word that is spelled the same but has different meanings that would fit all the blanks of the sentence and make sense. Insert the word in the blanks.*

1. When I was in the third _____, I received a low _____ in arithmetic.

2. Everytime I _____, I get a(n) _____ in my stockings.

3. I don't _____ _____ing my little brother because he has such a brilliant _____.

4. My basketball _____ said that he would _____ me in math while we were riding in the _____.

5. While riding our horses on the _____, we saw in _____ view a very _____ house.

6. He was a(n) _____ at the party because his _____ had won the game when he _____ the ball so hard.

7. It is the _____ of the custom officials to see to it that you pay _____ on certain things that are brought into the United States.

8. A(n) _____ of persons wearing a(n) _____ around their heads attacked our school _____.

9. I sit in a special _____ when I _____ the meeting.

10. When I take a test, I often _____ my _____ to make sure I do not run out of time.

Skill 11: Expanding Vocabulary with Homographs (Words That Are Spelled the Same but Have Different Meanings)

Exercise 4

Directions: *Read each sentence carefully. Think of a word that is spelled the same but has different meanings that would fit all the blanks of the sentence and make sense. Insert the word in the blanks.*

1. Whenever we _____ our car by the _____, we get a ticket.

2. The nice _____ said that his lips often _____ in cold weather.

3. At the _____, the _____ player dropped the ball right in the _____ of the court.

4. My brother _____ received a poor _____ when he _____ed the wrong answers.

5. The _____ said that he could give no _____ reason for having _____ed in political science.

6. I know a(n) _____ who owns a _____ whom he takes to every fight.

7. While sitting comfortably on the _____ing _____, I sipped my _____ in a leisurely way.

8. We gave the person who gave us a(n) _____ about a good stock a(n) _____ .

9. When the man with a high ranking _____ won the match, he gained the _____ to a large tract of land.

10. Mr. and Mrs. _____ always _____ their envelopes with the _____ of a(n) _____ .

Skill 11: Expanding Vocabulary with Homographs (Words That Are Spelled the Same but Have Different Meanings)

Exercise 5

Directions: *Read each sentence carefully. Think of a word that is spelled the same but has different meanings that would fit all the blanks of the sentence and make sense. Insert the word in the blanks.*

1. My mind goes _____ everytime I have to fill in any

   _____

2. In England, I paid two _____ for a book to help me shed

   some _____ .

3. The lawyer knew that he had won his _____ when he pro-

   duced the _____ containing the murder weapon.

4. A certain _____ of dogs is easier to _____ than

   others.

5. After he had drunk a lot of _____ he wasn't in very good

   _____ because he thought that he saw _____ .

6. Part of the _____ was to _____ a course no one

   could follow after we hid the jewels in the chosen cemetery

   _____ .

7. The police said that they would _____ everyone who was

   standing by the barbecue _____ at the time of the murder.

8. I always _____ by some _____ when I deliver a

   speech about my _____ on something.

9. I need to _____ up on the _____ structure of cer-

   tain animals for my biology examination.

10. Although I do not like to _____ opinions on what is proper

    _____ , I think that the _____ of the marriage

    service that you are planning should be changed.

Skill 11: Expanding Vocabulary with Homographs (Words That Are Spelled the Same but Have Different Meanings)

Exercise 6

Directions: *Read each sentence carefully. Think of a word that is spelled the same but has different meanings that would fit all the blanks of the sentence and make sense. Insert the word in the blanks.*

1. _____ your ticket to the man so that you can get into the _____ .

2. Although he was usually a(n) _____ runner, he did not run _____ after his long _____ , and he had difficulty in keeping a(n) _____ grip on the rope.

3. The _____ said that he would _____ the valuables with his life.

4. The newspaper _____ mentioned how a(n) _____ supporting a building had broken and fallen on a(n) _____ of soldiers.

5. The child said that she should receive a(n) _____ because she had been _____ all year.

6. My friends are good _____ , who enjoy _____ .

7. When we went to a famous _____ , we were able to _____ many well-known people there.

8. The woman standing under a(n) _____ was trying to _____ off some gems that she held in her _____ .

9. The _____ man said that we should _____ his name off the list because there was no _____ next to his name.

10. Although I am not in the _____ of wearing such a(n) _____ , it is the _____ here to wear one.

Skill 11: Expanding Vocabulary with Homographs (Words That Are Spelled the Same but Have Different Meanings)

Exercise 7

Directions: *Read each sentence carefully. Think of a word that is spelled the same but has different meanings that would fit all the blanks of the sentence and make sense. Insert the word in the blanks.*

1. The _____ maiden went to the _____ on a(n) _____ day.

2. My brother who is in _____ school gets very _____ grades.

3. I _____ the table every night in a(n) _____ way.

4. We used a(n) _____ to loosen the soil so that we could plant the seeds for the flowers that we would later _____.

5. I could not _____ my horn in the parade because a(n) _____ on my head had given me a headache.

6. He is a(n) _____ if he thinks that he can _____ you with that trick.

7. We have a(n) _____ in our lake that likes to _____ its head in the water.

8. _____ is always very _____ about everything he says.

9. Because I _____ easily when I swim, I like to have a tube from an old _____ on which to float.

10. Jane eats _____ while she _____ the trees.

Skill 11: Expanding Vocabulary with Homographs (Words That Are Spelled the Same but Have Different Meanings)

Exercise 8

Directions: *Read each sentence carefully. Think of a word that is spelled the same but has different meanings that would fit all the blanks of the sentence and make sense. Insert the word in the blanks.*

1. I wrote a(n) _____ to my friend of _____ telling her to _____ that she kept playing the wrong musical _____.

2. I like to read a(n) _____ with a(n) _____ plot.

3. My sister who is usually very _____ went into a(n) _____ when the dress she wanted did not _____.

4. I was feeling _____ until I saw the parking _____ that I had to pay.

5. His story _____s investigation because I do not believe that _____s usually their _____ for hunters.

6. The teacher asked the _____ to notice when the cat's _____ looked liked tiny slits.

7. When our dogs _____ a lot, we have them sleep in our out-door _____.

8. I became _____ when I saw that the _____ was painted a(n) _____ green rather than a bright yellow.

9. The _____ man always seems to break out in a(n) _____.

10. After the football player made a first _____, he fell _____ on what felt like a bed of _____.

Skill 11: Expanding Vocabulary with Homographs (Words That Are Spelled the Same but Have Different Meanings)

Exercise 9

Directions: *Read each sentence carefully. Think of a word that is spelled the same but has different meanings that would fit all the blanks of the sentence and make sense. (Although the words are spelled the same, they may or may not be pronounced the same.) Insert the word in the blanks.*

1. I am not _____ unless I know the _____ of the food I eat.

2. Because that is a(n) _____ idea, I will invest my _____ in your business, which is located in the _____ of Pennsylvania.

3. I have to _____ my dog not to bark when the _____ arrives because my dog interrupts my _____ of thought.

4. I cannot _____ unless I know that the _____ of the family is well taken care of.

5. Don't _____ that cane with its sharp _____ at me.

6. The _____ gave the _____ reason they would accept the terms.

7. To _____ a piece of music, I must first _____ myself.

8. I like to _____ horses of a certain _____ only.

9. Those persons _____ for the past three weeks, received my _____ .

10. It goes against my _____ to hear the price of _____ these days.

Skill 11: Expanding Vocabulary with Homographs (Words That Are Spelled the Same but Have Different Meanings)

Exercise 10

Directions: *Read each sentence carefully. Think of a word that is spelled the same but has different meanings that would fit all the blanks of the sentence and make sense. Insert the word in the blanks.*

1. The garden _____ made my _____ wet.

2. I felt _____ed after I spent hours trying to unclog the

   _____.

3. When my sister, _____, and I _____ in the morning, we saw that the first _____ in our _____ garden had bloomed.

4. Although dark clouds are usually a(n) _____ of rain, I continued to _____ the huge _____ that I had painted for the carnival party.

5. At the costume _____ we were surprised to see someone dressed as a(n) _____.

6. During a terrible _____ storm we were unable to _____ a cab.

7. Although she is _____, she likes to have her _____s open during the day.

8. After a number of _____ runs, the company decided that it would not have to put its plane on _____ anymore.

9. At the army _____ they usually _____ their decisions on what is best for the majority.

10. The murderer turned out to be a(n) _____ who always called the police and told them that he needed a(n) _____ to _____ up his car.

Skill 11: Expanding Vocabulary with Homographs (Words That Are Spelled the Same but Have Different Meanings)

Exercise 11

Directions: *Read each sentence carefully. Think of a word that is spelled the same but has different meanings that would fit all the blanks of the sentence and make sense. (Although the words are spelled the same, they may or may not be pronounced the same.) Insert the word in the blanks.*

1. I told them that I would _____ company from them unless they gave me a larger _____ in the play.

2. After I gave the guard my _____, I was told that I would have to _____ a number of security tests before I would be able to _____ through some of the areas.

3. _____, which is a city in France, is a(n) _____ place to visit.

4. The food left overnight in the _____ had _____ on it.

5. When my grandmother was playing _____, she developed an itch on the _____ of her nose, and at the same time, the _____ in her mouth came loose.

6. When the special regulatory agency _____ the pilot, who was supposedly _____ in all the fundamentals, they felt their decision was well _____.

7. The _____ of the experiment was to determine whether a person would _____ to being annoyed by strangers.

8. The person standing on the _____ said that she was not _____ing and that she intended to jump.

9. For our class _____, we are supposed to
_____ what we think education will be like in
the twenty-first century.

10. In my _____, I am in a(n) _____
to make my _____ on matters very clear.

Skill 11: Expanding Vocabulary with Homographs (Words That Are Spelled the Same but Have Different Meanings)

Exercise 12

Directions: *Read each set of phrases carefully. Think of a word that is spelled the same but has different meanings that would fit all the blanks in each set of phrases. Insert the word in the blanks.*

1. _____ call; jelly _____; _____ of wallpaper; _____ back; _____ up.

2. Flower _____; from _____ to stern; a goblet _____; _____ the leak.

3. A high _____; _____ card; four _____ and twenty; a musical _____.

4. _____ colors; _____ asleep; to break a(n) _____; run _____.

5. A(n) _____ person; to _____ someone; a(n) _____ fever; a(n) _____ amount.

6. _____ of a whip; _____ shut; not a(n) _____; _____ one's fingers at; a(n) _____ decision.

7. A(n) _____ decision; a skin _____.

8. A strong _____; _____ a ship.

9. _____ straw; at _____; _____ word; _____ night; the _____ person.

10. A monkey _____; to _____ free; to _____ a part of the body.

Skill 11: Expanding Vocabulary with Homographs (Words That Are Spelled the Same but Have Different Meanings)

Exercise 13

Directions: *Read each set of phrases carefully. Think of a word that is spelled the same but has different meanings that would fit all the blanks in each set of phrases. Insert the word in the blanks.*

1. Under one's _____; below the _____; _____ a person in the jaw; wear a(n) _____.

2. To _____; wear a(n) _____; to get a _____ out of someone's jokes; to give someone the _____, to be _____ed out; the player _____ed an easy grounder.

3. A cement _____ surrounding a grass plot; we were happy when we crossed the _____; Iowa _____s on Missouri; the _____ of the rug was done in a different color.

4. A(n) _____ drink; hard water _____s pipes; apply _____ to the land.

5. A baby _____; the _____ of a drum; they will probably _____ on for hours; the noise will probably _____ the players.

6. A(n) _____ person; a(n) _____ substance; a(n) _____ situation; _____land; a(n) _____ of racing cars; a(n) _____ of animals.

7. _____ it high; a chimney _____; a(n) _____ of money; a(n) _____ of paper; to _____ against someone; an air _____.

8. A low _____; a greenish _____; a moral _____; a pleasant _____.

9. To _____ into; a man's _____; to _____ the score; to _____ a knot.

10. _____ wind; a business _____; did a good _____; that is my _____; a(n) _____ route; a(n) _____ name.

Skill 11: Expanding Vocabulary with Homographs (Words That Are Spelled the Same but Have Different Meanings)

Exercise 14

Directions: *Read each set of phrases carefully. Think of a word that is spelled the same but has different meanings that would fit all the blanks in each set of phrases. Insert the word in the blanks.*

1. The _____ of the problem; a decayed _____; the _____ of all evil; the _____ of a word; the _____ of a tooth.

2. _____ at any chance; my _____ is broken; _____ your fingers; _____ the lock shut.

3. _____ the salad; I will _____ the report with research data.

4. _____ the bill; the _____ of the hill; on _____; the _____ of the bed.

5. _____ for an exam; _____ an ax; _____ her teeth; _____ out material.

6. The factory is in _____; the _____ was a success; it's a simple _____.

7. post _____; _____ water; a(n) _____ for animals; _____ out; the _____ of a typewriter; the _____ of a pail.

8. _____ the odds; the _____ is small; perfect _____.

9. Set in _____; a(n) _____ example; _____ poetry.

10. _____ out; an important _____; as a(n) _____; _____ a line; _____ a country.

Skill 11: Expanding Vocabulary with Homographs (Words That Are Spelled the Same but Have Different Meanings)

Exercise 15

Directions: *Read each set of phrases carefully. Think of a word that is spelled the same but has different meanings that would fit all the blanks in each set of phrases. Insert the word in the blanks.*

1. _____ it; a rolling _____; a hat _____; a bowling _____.

2. A(n) _____ of friendship; a strong _____; _____ paper; a savings _____.

3. A(n) _____ taste; live in a(n) _____; a(n) _____ drink; a(n) _____ rate; lying _____; _____ broke.

4. A(n) _____ man; a man of _____s; what I _____; arithmetic _____.

5. A bear _____; a mine _____; an orchestra _____; a peach _____.

6. A(n) _____ plant; a(n) _____ golf club; a baseball _____; a(n) _____ of water.

7. The _____ plan; wild _____; the _____ is up; a(n) _____ of skill; I'm _____; to make _____ of.

8. A(n) _____ for power; a(n) _____ for governor; a(n) _____ of people; a(n) _____ track; a(n) _____ horse.

9. _____ it on; take a different _____; a sharp _____.

10. _____ by _____; at the _____ of death; the boiling _____; a(n) _____ of departure; at the _____; _____ him out; the _____ of; the _____ of the matter; a sharp _____.

Skill 11: Expanding Vocabulary with Homographs (Words That Are Spelled the Same but Have Different Meanings)

Exercise 16

Directions: *Read each set of phrases carefully. Think of a word that is spelled the same but has different meanings that would fit all the blanks in each set of phrases. Insert the word in the blanks.*

1. A(n) _____ of beans; to _____ tomatoes; we _____ go.

2. To _____ animals; to ride a(n) _____.

3. _____ sense; _____ denominator; the _____ good.

4. A tuning _____; a(n) _____ in the road; to _____ over.

5. A walking _____; _____ a stamp on an envelope.

6. Beat him to the _____; _____ a picture.

7. A(n) _____ tree; to _____ for.

8. A boxing _____; _____ the bell.

9. To _____ a person in something; _____ payment.

10. _____ glass; license _____; dry the _____.

11. A(n) _____ of wolves; _____ your bags.

12. A car _____; a(n) _____ of water.

13. The large _____ of the college; _____ a garden.

14. An army _____; _____ the letter.

15. A(n) _____ of oxen; he or she _____ the car.

Skill 11: Expanding Vocabulary with Homographs (Words That Are Spelled the Same but Have Different Meanings)

Exercise 17

Directions: *Read each set of meanings carefully. Think of a word that is spelled the same but has different meanings that would fit each set of multiple meanings. Insert the word in the blank.*

Example: to cause to be different; small coins; another set of clothes

Answer: change

1. You do this to vote or when fishing; it can refer to actors in a play; it refers to a shade; if you break some parts of you, you're put into one.

   _____

2. A tree has this; a dog does this; it's also a small boat.

   _____

3. It's an insect; you do this to a kite; humans can't do this.

   _____

4. It's any bushy tail; it's a nation, it's a short, quick fight; it's sparsely settled country; you do this to your teeth. _____

5. It can be a long, round, slender piece of wood; it's a unit of measure; it refers to two places on opposite ends of the globe.

   _____

6. Without this part of your body you could not survive; it's a prominent position or being first in line; in music, it's the rounded part of a note; beer can have it; used in counting cattle. _____

7. It's a location; it's your job; it refers to your stand on some issue; it also refers to your status or rank. _____

8. It refers to a midpoint; it's a stingy person; it's something of slight value; however, in the plural, it's riches; moderation is this, too; it can refer to what you have in mind. _____

9. You can do this to a ball; it makes your speech interesting to listen to; it's also a black, sticky substance you wouldn't want on you.

   _____

10. It's sort of a handle used to start a machine; it can refer to shaky or unsteady; it's also a complaining person. _____

Skill 11: Expanding Vocabulary with Homographs (Words That Are Spelled the Same but Have Different Meanings)

Exercise 18

Directions: *Read each set of meanings carefully. Think of a word that is spelled the same but has different meanings that would fit each set of multiple meanings. Insert the word in the blank.*

Example: average; to have in mind; stingy

Answer: mean

1. A tool for writing; an enclosure for animals. _____

2. An admirer; a device for cooling the person.

   _____

3. A female domestic animal; a barrier preventing the flow of water.

   _____

4. A small missile; a quick movement; a stitched, tapering fold in a garment. _____

5. A male animal; to direct the course of transmission.

   _____

6. A device for gripping an object; a hold; part of an engine.

   _____

7. To smile with joy; heavy timber used in construction.

   _____

8. The young of an animal; to think gloomily.

   _____

9. A firm woven cloth usually made of wool and cotton; touched.

   _____

10. Equal in standing to another; gaze; a nobleman.

    _____

Skill 11: Expanding Vocabulary with Homographs (Words That Are Spelled the Same but Have Different Meanings)

Exercise 19

Directions: *Read each set of meanings carefully. Think of a word that is spelled the same but has different meanings that would fit each set of multiple meanings. Insert the word in the blank.*

Example: It refers to money but it can also begin a sentence; it is the seat of government but it can also mean "excellent."

Answer: capital

1. These help some to see better; you can drink out of them, too.

   _____

2. You can wear these, but someone does this after strenuous activity.

   _____

3. It can break up soil, can help you play your guitar, and helps you open your locked door; some persons do this to their food.

   _____

4. It's part of a ship; you can find one in school; it's used for building; it's the food for which you pay in an institution.

   _____

5. You can play this; you use it in sewing; you use it to bind something and use it for measuring. _____

6. You are this when you glow with color and health; it's also a flower.

   _____

7. It can be a character statement or a note in a book referring to another. _____

8. It's a bird, but it can be a machine, too. _____

9. Everyone does this when he or she writes his or her name; anyone can have some in front of his or her store; everyone reads lots of them when he or she travels on the highway. _____

10. This is alive, and it grows when you water it, but it can be a place in which you work. _____

11. It refers to a yard surrounded by buildings; cases are tried here; you do this when you woo someone. _____

12. A girl wears this, but it can be a small piece of paper, and you want to avoid doing this on ice. _____

13. You can take one in school; it's the path over which something moves; it's where you play golf. _____

14. It refers to someone who does not weigh a lot; it's not too important; you do this when you neglect or are disrespectful to someone.

_____

15. A ship has this; card players need this; it also means to cover or clothe with elegance. _____

Skill 11: Expanding Vocabulary with Homographs (Words That Are Spelled the Same but Have Different Meanings)

Exercise 20

Directions: *Read the sentences in each set carefully. Think of the word that is spelled the same but has different meanings that would fit the blank in the set. Insert the word in the blank. Define the word as it is used in each different sentence of each set.*

Set I

1. I have a(n) _____ in my stocking.
   _____

2. My brother will _____ for office in the next election. _____

3. Don't _____ so fast. _____

4. Let's give them a(n) _____ for their money.
   _____

Set II

1. At that _____ a waiter came to take our order.
   _____

2. What was your _____?
   _____

3. We went to the _____ for our vacation.
   _____

4. The _____ of the dagger scratched my arm.
   _____

Set III

1. What is the tax _____? _____

2. Play that in the major _____ of C.
   _____

3.. A fish has _____s. _____

4. Don't use that _____ to weigh yourself because it's broken. _____

Skill 12: Using Context Clues to Gain Word Meanings

Introduction and Examples*

By context we mean the words surrounding a word that can throw light on its meaning. You used context clues to help you figure out the meanings of homographs (words that are spelled the same but have different meanings.) Sentence context also helps you figure out words that are not homographs. For example, in the following sentence see if you can figure out the meaning of *hippodrome*.

> In ancient times the Greek people would assemble in their seats to observe the chariot races being held in the *hippodrome*.

From the context of the sentence, you should realize that *hippodrome* refers to some arena (place) where races were held in ancient Greece.

Sometimes you can actually gain the definition of the word from the sentence or following sentences. For example:

> The house had a cheerful atmosphere. At any moment I expected *blithe* spirits to make their entrance and dance with joy throughout the house.

From the sentences, you can determine that *blithe* refers to something joyful, gay, or merry.

Alert readers can also use contrasts or comparisons to gain clues to meanings of words. For example, try to determine the meaning of *ethereal* in the following sentence.

> He was impressed by the *ethereal* grace of Jane's walk rather than Ellen's heavy-footed one.

If you guessed *light, airy* for the meaning of *ethereal*, you were correct. You know that *ethereal* is somehow the opposite of *heavy*. This is an example of contrasts.

In the next example, see how comparisons can help you.

> Maria was as *fickle* as a politician's promises before election.

In this sentence *fickle* means "not firm in opinion" or "wavering." Because

*Dorothy Rubin, *Gaining Word Power* (New York: Macmillan, 1978).

politicians try to court all their constituents (voters) before an election, they often are not firm in their opinions, make many promises, and are wavering. By understanding the comparison, you can get an idea of the meaning of *fickle*.

In the following example notice how the words *that is* and its abbreviation *i.e.* usually signal that an explanation will follow.

Man is a biped, *that is,* an animal having only two feet.

or

Man is a biped, *i.e.*, an animal having only two feet.

Good readers use all these clues to help them determine word meanings.

Skill 12: Using Context Clues to Gain Word Meanings

Exercise 1

> Directions: *Read each sentence carefully. Use context clues to help you choose the word that* best *fits the sentence. A word may only be used once. (More words are given in the word list than you need.) Insert the word in the blank.*

Word List: buy, browse, pine, economy, suit, take, play, box, bore, pinch, coat, blade, post, rose, idle, work, iron, spectacles, posture, run, flowed, clothing, happy, fast, sell, dress

1. Good looks _____ in her family.
2. At the stadium the crowd _____ through the gate.
3. The pitcher was still in his or her _____.
4. At the library, I usually _____ through lots of books.
5. They said that they would try to _____ out their difficulties.
6. The children _____ for their dog who is missing.
7. During holidays, I usually feel the money _____.
8. Unless my mother wears her _____, she has difficulty seeing.
9. The senators surveyed the _____ of foreign affairs.
10. It is not good to allow your car motor to _____.
11. That color doesn't _____ you.
12. In our science class we examined a(n) _____ of grass under the microscope.
13. After she _____ from her chair, we noticed that she was hurt.
14. The carpenter _____ a hole in a classroom wall.
15. A number of people went on a(n) _____ to protest conditions at their place of work.

Skill 12: Using Context Clues to Gain Word Meanings

Exercise 2

Directions: *Read each sentence carefully. Read the word list. Use context clues to determine the feelings of the person in each sentence. Choose the word from the word list that best expresses the person's feelings. (All words fit in, and the word may be used only once.) Insert the word in the blank.*

Word List: ecstatic, disappointed, guilty, frustrated, anxious, peculiar, sad, embarrassed, ashamed, insulted

1. Judy was very _____ when her dress tore while she was reciting in front of the class.

2. I felt _____ when my favorite teacher left my school.

3. Jim, who had a sister, had wanted a brother for a long time. When his mother gave birth to twin girls, he was _____.

4. Jim felt _____ when he saw some of his classmates picking on younger children.

5. Carol was hoping that John would ask her to the dance. When John asked Carol to the dance, she was _____.

6. After working for two years on the housing proposal, Mr. Brown was very _____ when the board defeated the plan.

7. Kim felt _____ when she learned that she was the only one not invited to the party.

8. As Mike had never been in such a situation before, he felt

   _____.

9. Although I wasn't cheating, I felt _____ when the teacher said that someone was cheating.

10. Mary wanted to be on the swimming team. When the coach started to call the names of those who made it, she became very _____.

Skill 12: Using Context Clues to Gain Word Meanings

Exercise 3

Directions: *Using the context clues, determine the meaning of the underlined word as it is used in each sentence. Sometimes the clue to help you figure out the word meaning is in the next sentence. Write your answer in the space provided.*

1. In the alphabet, the letter *r* <u>precedes</u> the letter *s*.

   _____

2. Jane is the <u>recipient</u> of three science awards. She received the awards because of her work in controlling air pollution.

   _____

3. Mary plays a <u>dual</u> role in the play. In the first act she's a teen-ager, and in the second act she's middle-aged. _____

4. John is a very <u>conscientious</u> person; that is, he is very particular, thorough, and careful about everything he does. _____

5. It's interesting that in the same family you can have brothers and sisters, <u>siblings</u>, who are so different from one another.

   _____

6. Ellen has much more <u>stamina</u> than her sister Judy, who has no endurance for exertion. _____

7. When you <u>pilfer</u> something, you steal in small quantities or amounts.

   _____

8. He is a <u>candid</u> person; that is, he is always frank and open.

   _____

9. We didn't want Mr. Jones at our assembly because he is always so long-winded and <u>verbose</u>. _____

10. It seems odd to be <u>clad</u> in such heavy clothes in the month of July.

    _____

Skill 12: Using Context Clues to Gain Word Meanings

Exercise 4

Directions: *Each sentence has a nonsense word. Choose a word that you think would make sense in place of the nonsense word, and insert it in the blank. (Remember that you may choose any word you wish, but it must make sense in the sentence.)*

1. The grable _____ made us laugh and laugh.
2. When I was on the drein _____ I waved to all the people.
3. That is a cute slaible _____ you have.
4. Did you flan _____ all of that?
5. My favorite choy _____ is football.
6. We were slalled _____ when we learned that the picnic had been called off.
7. The firemen maibled _____ the boy from the burning building.
8. I enjoy talking on the whone _____.
9. No one would crake _____ to us.
10. The rostle _____ house frightened us.

Skill 12: Using Context Clues to Gain Word Meanings

Exercise 5

Directions: *Read the first sentence that has no scrambled words in it to get a clue to what the story is about. Then read very carefully each sentence that has a scrambled word or words in it. Using context clues, unscramble each word so that it makes sense in the story.*

In the forest there lived a kind old man and woman. *Hety*[1] have been *givinl*[2] here for *net*[3] years. They had *dovem*[4] to the *restof*[5] because life in their *tyci*[6] had become *oto*[7] much *rof*[8] them.

The *dink*[9] *lod*[10] man and woman *dame*[11] *treih*[12] living by *llnigse*[13] fresh *dekab*[14] *adesrb*[15] and *kaces*[16] to those *how*[17] came *ot*[18] *sivit*[19] the *restof*.[20] The *pluoce*[21] would *sola*[22] *elph*[23] *oneyna*[24] who *eeednd*[25] *ti*.[26] Everyone who *mace*[27] to *het*[28] forest *waysal*[29] visited *het*[30] old couple.

1. _____   11. _____   21. _____
2. _____   12. _____   22. _____
3. _____   13. _____   23. _____
4. _____   14. _____   24. _____
5. _____   15. _____   25. _____
6. _____   16. _____   26. _____
7. _____   17. _____   27. _____
8. _____   18. _____   28. _____
9. _____   19. _____   29. _____
10. _____   20. _____   30. _____

Skill 12: Using Context Clues to Gain Word Meanings

Exercise 6

Directions: *Read the first sentence that has no scrambled words in it to get a clue to what the story is about. Then read very carefully each sentence that has a scrambled word or words in it. Using context clues, unscramble each word so that it makes sense in the story.*

One day in mid-April we saw two ducks in our backyard. A while *altre*[1] we noticed some movement *nebaeht*[2] our Japanese *neip*[3] tree. A duck *dah*[4] built a(n) *stne*[5] under the *rete*.[6] In the nest *etreh*[7] were five *segg*.[8] The mother *kucd*[9] sat on *reh*[10] eggs every *yad*[11]. If anyone *amec*[12] near the *sent*,[13] the *thomer*[14] duck would *lapf*[15] her wings *nad*[16] start *kacniqgu*.[17] About *reteh*[18] weeks later *ew*[19] were *dwekaaen*[20] by lots of *osine*.[21] When we rushed *disetuo*,[22] we were *treedge*[23] by *vief*[24] little *luckingsd*[25] and their *roupd*[26] mother. The mother *kucd*[27] was *dealing*[28] her ducklings *ot*[29] a(n) *rmeast*.[30]

1. _____
2. _____
3. _____
4. _____
5. _____
6. _____
7. _____
8. _____
9. _____
10. _____

11. _____
12. _____
13. _____
14. _____
15. _____
16. _____
17. _____
18. _____
19. _____
20. _____

21. _____
22. _____
23. _____
24. _____
25. _____
26. _____
27. _____
28. _____
29. _____
30. _____

Skill 12: Using Context Clues to Gain Word Meanings

Exercise 7

Directions: *Read the title of this short story to get a clue to what the story is about. Then read very carefully each sentence that has a scrambled word or words in it. Using context clues, unscramble each word so that it makes sense in the story.*

THE RAT AND THE CAT

In our house we have an unusual *act*.[1] Our *act*[2] does not *tea*[3] *tsar*.[4] He *lapys*[5] with them. He only *teas*[6] *doof*[7] that we *tea*.[8] One day a *tar*[9] *mace*[10] to *vile*[11] in our *shueo*.[12] *Rou*[13] *act*[14] became *sit*[15] friend. When we set a *part*[16] for the *tar*,[17] *rou*[18] *act*[19] took a *keep*[20] at the *part*[21] and *was*[22] that he could *brag*[23] a *tibe*[24] of cheese from the *part*.[25] The *tar*[26] *sola*[27] wanted a *drawer*[28] so he too *koot*[29] a *tibe*[30] of cheese from the *part*.[31] After they ate, they *thob*[32] *koot*[33] a *pan*[34] *no*[35] the *pot*[36] of the *ternuoc*.[37] We *vener*[38] did *chatc*[39] any *tar*[40] in *rou*[41] *part*.[42]

1. _____	15. _____	29. _____
2. _____	16. _____	30. _____
3. _____	17. _____	31. _____
4. _____	18. _____	32. _____
5. _____	19. _____	33. _____
6. _____	20. _____	34. _____
7. _____	21. _____	35. _____
8. _____	22. _____	36. _____
9. _____	23. _____	37. _____
10. _____	24. _____	38. _____
11. _____	25. _____	39. _____
12. _____	26. _____	40. _____
13. _____	27. _____	41. _____
14. _____	28. _____	42. _____

Skill 12: Using Context Clues to Gain Word Meanings

Exercise 8

Directions: *Read the first sentence of the story to get a clue to what the story is about. Then read each sentence that has a missing word or words very carefully. Using context clues, insert a word in each blank so that the story makes sense.*

In the year 2022 many families live on the moon. Life on the
(1)_____ is a great (2)_____ different
(3)_____ earth (4)_____. To give (5)_____
an idea (6)_____ life (7)_____ the moon, let's follow
Alison, a nine-(8)_____-old. Most (9)_____ Alison
awakens (10)_____ 7:00 A.M. Moontime. (11)_____
puts on (12)_____ special moonsuit (13)_____ moon-
shoes, and then she goes to (14)_____ community bathroom.
(You see, everyone (15)_____ the (16)_____ lives
together in (17)_____ huge bubblelike enclosure.) In
(18)_____ community bathroom, Alison enters
(19)_____ special room in which she (20)_____ off
her moon (21)_____. After (22)_____ bath, Alison
redresses (23)_____ goes to the large community social
(24)_____ to meet with (25)_____ family
(26)_____ plan for the day. Alison wonders (27)_____
exciting (28)_____ she (29)_____ do
(30)_____ learn today.

Skill 12: Using Context Clues to Gain Word Meanings

Exercise 9

Directions: *Read the first sentence of the story to get a clue to what the story is about. Then read each sentence that has a missing word or words very carefully. Using context clues, insert a word in each blank so that the story makes sense.*

Everyone was looking forward to Friday night because that was the night of the big basketball game. This (1)_____ would determine the championship (2)_____ Deerville High and Yorkstown (3)_____. For years Deerville High and (4)_____ High have been rivals. This (5)_____ was very (6)_____ because so far (7)_____ school had won (8)_____ equal number of games. (9)_____ game on Friday night would break the (10)_____.

Friday night finally arrived. The game (11)_____ the championship title (12)_____ being played in the Deerville High (13)_____ because the game (14)_____ year had been played (15)_____ the Yorktown high gym. (16)_____ gym was so (17)_____ that many spectators were without (18)_____. When the two teams (19)_____ the gym from the dressing areas (20)_____ were thunderous (21)_____ and whistles from the (22)_____. Each team went through (23)_____ warm-up drills of (24)_____ baskets and passing. Then the buzzer (25)_____. The game would begin (26)_____ a moment. Just as the referee (27)_____ the ball in the (28)_____ for the starting jumpball, the lights (29)_____ the gym went (30)_____. There was complete darkness. Everyone (31)_____ taken by surprise. Almost immediately a (32)_____ on the loudspeaker (33)_____ that the game would have (34) _____ be postponed because of a (35) _____ failure. The game would take (36) _____ next Friday. All were (37) _____ to remain where they (38) _____ until someone with a flashlight came to help them.

Skill 12: Using Context Clues to Gain Word Meanings

Exercise 10

Directions: *Read each sentence* carefully. *Read the words in the word list. Use context clues to help you choose the word that best fits the sentence. (More words are given in the word list than you need.) Insert the word in the blank.*

Word List: gruesome, dreary, means, constant, fatigue, tender, crafty, segregated, lethal, firm, frustrated, ecstasy, verbose, brief, tactful, overt, covert, fine, internal, inquisitive, capital

1. Albany is the _____ of New York State.

2. He was in a state of _____ when the home-coming queen said that she would go to the dance with him.

3. I was told to give a(n) _____ speech after dinner rather than a long-winded one.

4. I dislike _____ people who ask a lot of questions.

5. A karate expert's hands are considered a(n) _____ weapon.

6. I tried not to be _____ when my plan was defeated.

7. We like everything to be aboveboard and open rather than _____.

8. Because Maria does not like to hurt anyone's feelings, she is trying to think of a _____ way to tell Joe that he wasn't chosen to be on the team.

9. After working so hard today, I should be in a state of _____, but I'm not.

10. What a(n) _____ person he was; he deceived everyone.

Name _____ Class _____ Date _____

Skill 13: Expanding Vocabulary with Synonyms and Antonyms

Introduction and Examples

Synonyms are different words that have almost the same meaning. Often words may be defined by other words of similar and more familiar meaning. For example, *malady,* is defined as *illness,* and *grave* is defined as *serious.*

The word *or* may be used by the writer when he or she uses another word or words with a similar meaning.

Example: John said that he felt ill after having eaten *rancid* or *spoiled* butter.

Antonyms are words opposite in meaning to others. *Examples:* fat, thin; worst, best; tall, short. Many times such words as *but, yet, however,* and *rather than* signal that a contrast or opposite is being used. Example: We always thought that a certain family was quite poor, but we just learned that they are actually quite *affluent.* (From the sentence you can tell that *affluent* is the opposite of *poor*; therefore *affluent* means "not poor" but "wealthy" or "rich.")

Authors use antonyms in contrast sentences to help make their writing more interesting, more informative, and clearer.

157

Skill 13: Expanding Vocabulary with Synonyms

Exercise 1

Directions: *Read each sentence carefully. Read the words in the word list. Choose the word that is similar in meaning to the underlined word in the sentence. (More words are given than you need. A word may be used only once.)*

Word List: tired, full, good, tense, funny, thin, large, small, tremendous, journey, drowsy, perilous, plump, new, snug, location, well-known, head, admired, passage, cheerful, near

1. That is a big house. _____
2. The chubby baby is eating a banana. _____
3. I was standing close to my famous friend. _____
4. I feel so sleepy. _____
5. This dress is too tight on me. _____
6. We found the package at the top of the stairs.

   _____
7. They went on a trip to California. _____
8. Where is that place? _____
9. Something blocked our way. _____
10. The mountain path looked very dangerous to me.

    _____

Skill 13: Expanding Vocabulary with Synonyms

Exercise 2

Directions: *Read each sentence carefully. Read the words in the word list. Choose the word that is similar in meaning to the underlined word in the sentence. (More words are given than you need. A word may be used only once.)*

Word List: nice, favorite, wizard, scent, healthy, content, wealthy, jeopardy, scream, raze, career, significant, posture, mean, notorious, exterior, flinch, special, grave, stink

1. The <u>odor</u> was very strong. _____
2. After dinner everyone appeared very <u>satisfied</u>.

   _____
3. She is an <u>expert</u> in math. _____
4. Al Capone was an <u>infamous</u> criminal. _____
5. His military <u>carriage</u> was upright and stiff.

   _____
6. The crew will <u>demolish</u> the old building tomorrow.

   _____
7. She had a very <u>serious</u> illness. _____
8. They knew that their lives were in <u>danger</u>. _____
9. They didn't even <u>cringe</u> when the gunman waved his pistol at them.

   _____
10. That was an <u>important</u> discovery. _____

Skill 13: Expanding Vocabulary with Synonyms

Exercise 3

Directions: *Read each sentence carefully. Read the words in the word list. Choose the word that is similar in meaning to the underlined word in the sentence. (All words fit in.)*

Word List: immature, equivalent, huge, group, remedy, capital, intimidate, sufficient, exhausted, annual

1. That is a large building. _____
2. She is tired from the ten-mile hike. _____
3. We have equal amounts. _____
4. Our school holds its yearly picnic in the spring.

   _____

5. You need money to start a business. _____
6. I think that is enough . _____
7. The flock of birds lived together on the farm.

   _____

8. Her behavior is very childish . _____
9. You cannot frighten me. _____
10. I don't think that there is a cure for the common cold.

    _____

Skill 13: Expanding Vocabulary with Synonyms

Exercise 4

Directions: *Read each sentence carefully. Read the words in the word list. Choose the word that is similar in meaning to the underlined phrase. (More words are given than you need. A word may be used only once.)*

Word List: frozen, icy, torrid, discreet, affluent, spectacular, verbose, frigid, exhausted, obese, famished, ecstatic, diligent, ancient, terse, immense, anxiety, remorseful, skinny, potent, anxious, brilliant, beautiful

1. My sister is very pretty. _____
2. The girl is very thin. _____
3. After the trip we were very hungry. _____
4. After the long journey we were very tired. _____
5. The very smart student won a scholarship. _____
6. The very fat circus lady wore a tent for a dress.

   _____
7. The very powerful medicine knocked me out.

   _____
8. The very wealthy man owns a mansion. _____
9. She is very happy. _____
10. She is a very hardworking person. _____
11. His speech was very brief. _____
12. Famous people must be very careful about what they do or say.

    _____
13. It is very cold in the North Pole. _____
14. It was a very unusual scene. _____
15. That is a very large building. _____

Skill 13: Expanding Vocabulary with Synonyms

Exercise 5

Directions: *Read each phrase carefully. Read the words in the word list. Place the word beside the phrase that is similar in meaning to it. (All words will be used.)*

Word List: emaciated, satiated, exhausted, ancient, brilliant, posthaste, dogged, saturated, parched, obese, huge, torrid

1. very hot _____
2. very tired _____
3. very smart _____
4. very large _____
5. very fat _____
6. very old _____
7. very full _____
8. very wet _____
9. very dry _____
10. very thin _____
11. very fast _____
12. very determined _____

Skill 13: Expanding Vocabulary with Synonyms

Exercise 6

Directions: *Read the first word at the beginning of each set. Read the words in each set. Circle the word in each set that is most similar in meaning to the word at the beginning of the set. (You may use the dictionary to help you.)*

1. famished: (a) tired, (b) exhausted, (c) starved, (d) finished
2. content: (a) joyful, (b) certain, (c) reasonable, (d) satisfied
3. arrogant: (a) haughty, (b) prudish, (c) passionate, (d) ignorant
4. thrifty: (a) cheap, (b) wasteful, (c) economical, (d) stingy
5. prudent: (a) priggish, (b) snobbish, (c) proper, (d) wise
6. modify: (a) change, (b) clarify, (c) model, (d) please
7. dire: (a) friendly, (b) helpful, (c) extreme, (d) noticeable
8. succinct: (a) shorten, (b) concise, (c) curious, (d) exaggerated
9. covet: (a) hide, (b) expose, (c) desire, (d) law
10. curtail: (a) sharpen, (b) save, (c) salvage, (d) shorten
11. postpone: (a) delay, (b) think, (c) prepare, (d) choose
12. inclining: (a) closeness, (b) leaning, (c) caring, (d) property

Skill 13: Expanding Vocabulary with Synonyms

Exercise 7

Directions: *Read the first word at the beginning of each set. Read the words in each set. Choose the word in each set that is most similar in meaning to the word at the beginning of the set. (You may use the dictionary to help you.)*

1. discipline: (a) praise, (b) punish, (c) hold, (d) sing
2. fate: (a) mistake, (b) open, (c) secret, (d) destiny
3. cohere: (a) stick, (b) inhabit, (c) mix, (d) produce
4. oblivious: (a) frightened, (b) forgetful, (c) erasing, (d) worried
5. obliterate: (a) decimate, (b) forget, (c) erase, (d) mar
6. exodus: (a) immigration, (b) immigrant, (c) emigration, (d) export
7. dubious: (a) inserting, (b) knowledgeable, (c) false, (d) doubtful
8. credible: (a) credit, (b) believable, (c) pausing, (d) delaying
9. fraud: (a) assistant, (b) clown, (c) magician, (d) faker
10. forlorn: (a) miserable, (b) silent, (c) forgotten, (d) departed
11. craving: (a) false, (b) invalid, (c) convincing, (d) desiring
12. caution: (a) hope, (b) cause, (c) warn, (d) stop

Skill 13: Expanding Vocabulary with Antonyms

Exercise 8

Directions: *Read each sentence carefully. Read the words in the word list. Choose the word that is opposite in meaning to the underlined word in the sentence, and place it in the blank. (More words are given than you need. A word may be used only once.)*

Word List: clear, less, cleanest, short, shortest, more, greatest, complex, most, worst, wordy, naive, helpful, cheerful, old, vain, fast, fastest, nice, friendly, modern, tame, similar, ferocious, diseased

1. My brother is the <u>tallest</u> basketball player on the team.

   _____

2. They did the <u>least</u> work. _____

3. That was the <u>best</u> basketball game I've ever seen.

   _____

4. She ate <u>more</u> ice cream than I did. _____

5. That is the <u>dirtiest</u> shirt that I have ever seen.

   _____

6. That is the <u>slowest</u> train that I have ever been on.

   _____

7. I like <u>wild</u> animals. _____

8. That is not a <u>simple</u> problem. _____

9. That is an <u>ancient</u> custom. _____

10. What a <u>sophisticated</u> person she is! _____

165

Skill 13: Expanding Vocabulary with Antonyms

Exercise 9

Directions: *Read each sentence carefully. Read the words in the word list. Choose the word that is opposite in meaning to the underlined word in the sentence, and place it in the blank. (More words are given than you need. A word may be used only once.)*

Word List: dark, clear, confusing, fickle, happy, talkative, densely, brief, different, curtail, proud, humble, stupid, tense, punctual, foolhardy, polite, prudent, severe, mean, sorry, friendly

1. That is a <u>lucid</u> statement. _____
2. She is a <u>rash</u> person. _____
3. He is the most <u>conceited</u> person I know. _____
4. Make sure the dresses are <u>uniform</u>. _____
5. His talks are usually too <u>verbose</u>. _____
6. My friend is always <u>late</u>. _____
7. My area is <u>sparsely</u> populated. _____
8. My cousin is a <u>rude</u> person. _____
9. Is it possible to <u>prolong</u> the meeting? _____
10. He is a <u>true</u> friend. _____

Skill 13: Expanding Vocabulary with Antonyms

Exercise 10

Directions: *Read the first word at the beginning of each set. Read the words in each set. Circle the word in each set that is opposite in meaning to the word at the beginning of the set. (Use the dictionary to help you.)*

1. less: (a) most, (b) least, (c) great, (d) more
2. significant: (a) important, (b) unimportant, (c) meaningful, (d) dreadful
3. terminate: (a) end, (b) begin, (c) final, (d) settle
4. covert: (a) open, (b) frightened, (c) closed, (d) secretive
5. impotent: (a) powerless, (b) heavy, (c) powerful, (d) empty
6. optimist: (a) friendly, (b) pessimist, (c) cheerful, (d) happy
7. temperate: (a) moderate, (b) mild, (c) excessive, (d) restrained
8. candid: (a) happy, (b) joyful, (c) evasive, (d) frank
9. sophisticated: (a) wise, (b) worldly, (c) silly, (d) naive
10. terse: (a) brief, (b) succinct, (c) verbose, (d) tough
11. hyperbolic: (a) understated, (b) exaggerated, (c) excessive, (d) little
12. erratic: (a) wandering, (b) peculiar, (c) errors, (d) stable

section three

Fun with Words:
Word Riddles and
Word Puzzles

Word Riddles 1

See how many of the word riddles you can solve.

1. I'm a five-letter word that hangs nicely in the living room; remove two letters, and I can climb trees. _____ _____

2. I'm what you can do with crayons; add a letter, and I become a Southerner's way of speaking. _____ _____

3. I can be a small cut; add two letters, and I become small change. _____ _____

4. I'm what you call a group of certain animals; if you remove one of my letters, I am something you can do to a door. _____ _____

Word Riddles 2

See how many of the word riddles you can solve.

1. I'm yellow and go great with hot dogs. Take away my last three letters, and I mean the same as "have to." What am I? _____

   _____

2. I'm the opposite of *open*, but if you add a *t*, I hold your clothes. What am I? _____ _____

3. I'm a five-letter word that contains lots of love. Take the vowels out, and replace them with another, and this is what pain does.

   _____ _____

4. From a six-letter word meaning rug, remove the second syllable, and you get something you can drive. _____ _____

5. To a four-letter word for what you do with a song, add a letter at the end, and get a word that means "to burn the edge." _____

   _____

Word Riddles 3

See how many of the word riddles you can solve.

1. My first word is something you ring. My second word is the opposite of *girl*. Put us together, and you have someone who carries things.
   _____ _____ _____

2. My first word is a color. My second word is something that flies. Put us together, and you have my name. _____ _____
   _____

3. You can put things in my first word, and you can read my second. Put us together, and you have something that holds lots of things.
   _____ _____ _____

4. My first word is used to make drinks cold. My second word is the solid part of the earth's surface. Put us together, and you have the name of a country. _____ _____ _____

5. My first word comes from the sky. My second word you can wear in your hair. Put us together, and you have a beautiful arc of many different colors. _____ _____ _____

Word Riddles 4

See how many of the word riddles you can solve.

1. When you remove one letter from a four-letter word meaning "in the back," you have what you hear with. _____ _____

2. Add one letter to something you can't live without, and you will have something you brush. _____ _____

3. When you finish eating this five-letter word, remove one letter, and you can do it to a book. _____ _____

4. Add three letters to frozen water, and you have community helpers.

   _____ _____

5. This groom removed one letter from something that leads his horse, and he found the person he was looking for. _____ _____

6. Remove the last letter from a six-letter word in which you hang things, and you have the opposite of *far*. _____ _____

7. Change the first letter of a three-letter word of an animal that eats a lot, and you have a rhyming word meaning the opposite of *little*.

   _____ _____

Word Riddles 5

See how many of the word riddles you can solve.

1. Add one letter to frozen water, and you have what you throw at weddings. _____ _____

2. Take away the last two letters from the little boy you find on Valentine cards, and you have something you can drink out of. _____

   _____

3. Add the opposite of *off* to what a goat does, and you have something that fits through a hole. _____ _____

4. Remove two letters from a relative, and you have watery soup.

   _____ _____

5. Add two letters to an insect, and you have something that grows.

   _____ _____

6. Remove the last two letters of a five-letter word for cloth your jeans are usually made of, and you have an animal's house. _____

   _____

7. When you remove one letter from something that travels in water, it becomes a reptile. _____ _____

8. You will have a coin when you remove one letter from a word that means odor. _____ _____

9. Remove the last syllable from another word for rabbit, and you have something good to ear. _____ _____

10. You can write with this, but if you add a syllable to it, you have a small coin. _____ _____

Word Riddles 6

See how many of the word riddles you can solve.

1. I rhyme with *joke*, but if you change two letters, you'll find me in an egg. _____ _____

2. I'm round and represent the world, but you can take away one letter, and I'll become part of your ear. _____ _____

3. I'm a beautiful large bird, but when you take away my last syllable, I become a vegetable. _____ _____

4. I like to climb trees and eat bananas, but when you take away my first syllable, I can turn only in a lock. _____ _____

5. I grow in dampness or decay, and people avoid eating me; when you take away one of my letters, you have another reason for my condition. _____ _____

Word Riddles 7

See how many of the word riddles you can solve.

1. I am round, light, and I float in the air. If you take away my last three letters, I am better for bouncing. _____ _____

2. I am a five-letter word for what some persons can grow on their faces. Take away two letters, and you have a part of your head.

   _____ _____

3. Smart people have lots of this. When you remove two of its letters, it falls from the sky. _____ _____

4. I am good to lie on, and when you take away two letters that are in the word that is the opposite of *high*, I can help you get better.

   _____ _____

5. This insect likes your clothes. If you add two letters to it, you will get rid of it and get an important person. _____

   _____

Word Riddles 8

See how many of the word riddles you can solve.

1. I'm good to eat, but if you take away one letter, I become part of your head. _____ _____

2. Cereal is made out of them, but if you add one letter, you can travel on water in them. _____

   _____

3. I make this sound when I'm hurt, but if you add one letter, you can sit on me. _____ _____

4. You can stay in me, but if you get bored, you can take away the last two letters and drive away. _____

   _____

5. I'm part of a tree, but if you take away my first letter, you can breed cattle here. _____

   _____

Word Riddles 9

See how many of the word riddles you can solve.

1. It's part of my body; add one letter to it, and it's a place where you grow food. _____ _____

2. You do this with your eyes; take away one letter, and I become part of a chain. _____ _____

3. I'm a unit of length; add a letter to me, and I become something accomplished very easily. _____ _____

4. This place is nice to look at and to visit; take away one letter, and you can sail away in it; add another letter to it, and it can fly away.

   _____ _____ _____

5. I can be a part of either a tree or a person; add one letter to me, and I become something that goes upward, or I serve as a means of going up or higher. _____ _____

6. I am a small, short-legged pet; take away one of my letters, and I become a large bird of prey. _____ _____

Word Riddles 10

See how many of the word riddles you can solve.

1. I'm a joker who makes you laugh; take away my two beginning letters and add two different ones. Now you know what I do if I don't make you laugh. _____ _____

2. I'm used as a spice; take away one of my letters, and you may have the "spice of life." _____ _____

3. I'm another word for *boy;* add one letter to me, and I'll be happy.
_____ _____

4. I'm what you do when you're in a hurry; add two letters to the beginning of me, and I become a bird. _____
_____

Word Riddles 11

See how many of the word riddles you can solve.

1. I'm something you use for weaving; add a letter to me, and I become something that attracts bees. _____
   _____

2. I'm used to tie things together; take away one of my letters, and you will think that you're seeing double. _____
   _____

3. I'm sinister and not well-liked; add one letter to me, and you'll know who causes me. _____ _____

4. I'm a thick dark substance that's hard to get off; take away one of my letters, and you'll know what'll happen to you if you get stuck in me.

   _____ _____

Name _____ Class _____ Date _____

Word Riddles 12

See how many of the word riddles you can solve.

1. I'm what you take when you're ill; take away one of my letters, and I can cover your floor. _____ _____

2. My first word is the name of a tree; my second is what a plane does at the end of a flight. Put us together, and I become a city in California. _____ _____ _____

3. My first word refers to pulling something along; my second is the opposite of *off*. Put us together, and watch out. _____ _____ _____

4. When I do this, I can be very irritating; take away one of my letters, and I will be free from pain or discomfort. _____ _____

5. I'm the past tense of *ride*. Put one letter in front of me, and I'll slowly wear away. _____ _____

182

Word Riddles 13

See how many of the word riddles you can solve.

1. My first word is the home of a wild animal; my second word is what teachers do to test papers. Put us together, and I become a country.

   _____ _____ _____

2. My first word helps you to get away; my second word means the same as *decay*. Put us together, and you have a vegetable. _____

   _____ _____

3. My first word is another way of saying, "Mother"; my second word refers to small insects. Put us together, and you have the opposite of *charity*. _____ _____ _____

4. My first word is a metric unit; my second word means "to spoil." Put us together, and you'll have a subject that is studied in school.

   _____ _____ _____

Word Riddles 14

See how many of the word riddles you can solve.

1. My first word is the opposite of *old,* and my second word is a boat or ship. Put us together, and you have a city. _____
   _____   _____

2. My first word means "to make a mistake," and my second word is a conjunction that is often used. Put us together, and you will send someone on a short trip for another. _____   _____
   _____

3. My first word is a baby goat, and my second word is what you do when you're tired. Put us together, and act quickly to prevent a crime.
   _____   _____   _____

4. My first word is something you wear on your head; my second word is a cereal grass. Put us together, and you have the opposite of *steadfastness.* _____   _____   _____

Word Riddles 15

See how many of the word riddles you can solve.

1. I'm a four-letter word that is necessary for flying; add one letter to me, and you, too, can almost fly. _____ _____

2. I'm something a football player does; I'm used for building, and children can play with me. Take away one of my letters, and I'll help keep you safe. _____ _____

3. I am the opposite of *former*; add one letter to me, and you can use me for serving. _____ _____

4. I'm a four-letter word that you use to shoo away an animal; take away one of my letters, and I become one of the animals. _____

   _____

5. I mean "lean" or "slender"; add one letter to me, and I become an empty space. _____ _____

Word Riddles 16

See how many of the word riddles you can solve.

1. I'm what you eat from; if you take away one of my letters, I'll never be on time. _____   _____

2. I absorb moisture; remove two of my letters, and I'm what you need if your car gets stuck. _____

   _____

3. I'm found in a shell, and I'm good to eat; if you add one letter to me, I can fasten things. _____

   _____

4. I'm what a worker likes to get if he or she does a good job; remove one of my letters, and I become something a worker likes even more.

   _____   _____

5. I'm a resting place for wild animals; add three letters to me, and I become a young, unmarried woman. _____

   _____

6. We are persons with mysterious power; add one letter, and you will know our power. _____

   _____

Word Riddles 17

See how many of the word riddles you can solve.

1. I mean "to go upward with continuous progress"; take away one of my letters, and you'll have something that helps me go upward.

   _____   _____

2. I'm a wild animal of the dog family; take away one of my letters, and I become a domesticated work animal. _____

   _____

3. I'm usually a mischievous child; add one letter to me, and you'll make me spiritless or exhausted. _____

   _____

4. I'm a four letter word meaning "girl"; add a letter to me, and I become a member of high social rank. _____

   _____

Word Riddles 18

See how many of the word riddles you can solve.

1. I'm a female deer; add one letter to me, and I'll become a bird.

   _____ _____

2. I'm an animal; add one letter to me, and I'll grow on some faces.

   _____ _____

3. I'm a cooling device; add one letter to me, and I'll become a sharp weapon of animals. _____ _____

4. I'm a beverage; add one letter to me, and I'll become a hardy cabbage.

   _____ _____

5. I'm a tall grass; add one letter to me, and I'll have an excessive desire to own things. _____ _____

Word Riddles 19

Below are four sets of riddles. One word fits each set of riddles. Find the word.

1. A girl sometimes wears this. A criminal tries to give this to the police. You can get hurt if you do this. _____

2. I can make things brighter. I am part of a camera. I help plants develop. _____

3. Police do this to get information. You can cook on this. You can eat in this. _____

4. I'm a weight and a shoe; I can also stop progress. You hate it when I do this to your sink. _____

Word Riddles 20

Below are four sets of riddles. One word fits each set of riddles. Find the word.

1. I'm something used in combat that moves; I'm also a huge container.
   _____

2. I'm part of you that can be broken; I'm a cut of beef; I'm the primary vein of a leaf. When I want to, I can be a "joke." _____

3. I'm something you can wear, and I'm a piece of land jutting out into the water. _____

4. I can help to keep you safe; I'm the explanation to a riddle; I'm a clue to something; I'm part of a musical instrument; I'm a low island or reef; I'm of basic importance. _____

Word Puzzles 21

Following are eight clues for eight three-letter words.
(Hint: Each word begins and ends with the same letter.)

_____ 1. A young dog.

_____ 2. Another way of saying, "Father."

_____ 3. A young child.

_____ 4. An organ found in humans and animals.

_____ 5. A practical joke.

_____ 6. A female sheep.

_____ 7. A baby wears this.

_____ 8. A person devoted to a religious life.

Word Puzzles 22

Below are ten clues for ten words. After you guess the first word, the last two letters of each preceding word begin your next word. (Note that the number of spaces is also a clue to the number of letters in the word.)

1. You read about news in a _ _ _ _ _ _.
2. You use this to rub out something. _ _ _ _ _ _ _
3. When you make a mistake, you make an _ _ _ _ _ _.
4. Something new is _ _ _ _ _ _ _ _ _.
5. When no one is with you, you are _ _ _ _ _ _.
6. A bird builds a _ _ _ _ _.
7. You can see this at night when the sky is clear. _ _ _ _ _
8. A subject in school dealing with numbers. _ _ _ _ _ _ _ _ _ _ _
9. When water freezes, you get _ _ _.
10. Another word for *penny*. _ _ _ _ _

Word Puzzles 23

Below are 15 clues for 15 words. After you guess the first word, the last two letters of each preceding word begin the next word.

1. You put this at the end of a sentence. _____
2. This is another word for *scent*. _____
3. This is a fruit. _____
4. This is the opposite of *harsh*. _____
5. This is a citrus fruit. _____
6. This is a number. _____
7. This is the opposite of *always*. _____
8. This is another word for *mistake*. _____
9. This is a bird. _____
10. *A* is one. _____
11. This refers to a time period in history. _____
12. This is a dried fruit sometimes found in cereal. _____
13. This refers to one time only. _____
14. This means "to stop doing something." _____
15. This refers to the line where stitches are joined. _____

Word Puzzles 24

Below are 16 clues for 16 words. After you guess the first word, the last two letters of each preceding word begin the next word.

1. A fruit with yellow skin. _____
2. That by which a person is known. _____
3. Solid food. _____
4. A person trained in sports. _____
5. To annoy someone. _____
6. A line formed from sewing. _____
7. To entertain. _____
8. A school term. _____
9. Unstable. _____
10. Frozen water. _____
11. Period of 100 years. _____
12. A grain. _____
13. The day before today. _____
14. A way of saying, "Yes." _____
15. Color of the sun. _____
16. A nocturnal bird. _____

Word Puzzles 25

After you figure out the first word, each direction and each clue are based on the preceding word.

1. Polite persons use this word. _____

2. Remove one letter from item 1, and you have what you sign when you rent an apartment. _____

3. Change one letter from item 2, and you have the opposite of *most*. _____

4. Remove one letter from item 3, and you have a direction. _____

5. Add one letter to item 4, and you have a large, four-footed animal. _____

6. Change one letter from item 5, and you have an elaborate meal with lots to eat. _____

7. Remove one letter from item 6, and you have the opposite of *slow*. _____

8. Change one letter from item 7, and you have the opposite of *first*. _____

9. Change one letter from item 8, and you have another word for *girl*. _____

10. Add one letter to item 9, and you have what you drink out of. _____

11. Change one letter in item 10, and you have a word for "a group of students taught together." _____

Word Puzzles 26

Below are ten clues for ten words. After you guess the first word, the last letter of that word will be the first letter of the next word.

1. A male animal. _____
2. A long, slimy, snakelike fish. _____
3. The king of beasts. _____
4. A bad dream. _____
5. A tree. _____
6. A representation of an area. _____
7. Part of your hand. _____
8. A large, impressive residence. _____
9. A fruit. _____
10. A huge animal. _____

Word Puzzles 27

Fill in the spaces to make 15 four-letter words. To help you, a clue and a letter are given for each word.

1. The opposite of *short*. — a — —
2. It flies. — i — —
3. The opposite of *fat*. — h — —
4. The opposite of *sad*. — l — —
5. The opposite of *up*. — o — —
6. A girl wears this. — l — —
7. This is good to eat. — a — —
8. You can ride this. — i — —
9. A fast animal. — e — —
10. A grain. — i — —
11. A vegetable. — e — —
12. A fruit. — e — —
13. A long, slender, creeping animal. — o — —
14. An evergreen tree. — i — —
15. All plants have this. — o — —

Word Puzzles 28

The following clues help you figure out the four-letter words to which they refer. Start at item 1, and go on changing only one letter in each word to make a new word that fits the clue.

1. A season. _____
2. You bounce this. _____
3. Lacking hair on the head. _____
4. A large package of pressed-together material. _____
5. A story. _____
6. A man or boy. _____
7. An enclosed shopping center. _____
8. Where grain is ground into flour. _____
9. Equal to 5,280 feet or 1,609.3 meters. _____
10. A small, burrowing animal. _____
11. Something formed or shaped in or on. _____
12. A precious metal. _____
13. Game played with a small, hard rubber ball. _____
14. The animal Little Red Riding Hood meets. _____

Word Puzzles 29

The following clues help you figure out the five-letter words to which they refer. Start at item 1, and go on changing only one letter in each word to make a new word that fits the clue.

1. This goes around a picture. _____

2. A tongue of light rising from a fire. _____

3. To find fault with. _____

4. A fire. _____

5. To give a hard, smooth, glossy finish to. _____

6. Cows do this in a field of grass. _____

7. You do this to tests. _____

8. An occupation. _____

9. You do this when you copy letters by drawing lines around them.

_____

10. A mark left by a person or animal. _____

11. To break or split. _____

Word Puzzles 30

Below are 15 clues for 15 words. After you guess the first word, the last two letters of each preceding word begin the next word.

1. A piece of land for growing things. _____
2. The opposite of *exit*. _____
3. To get rid of writing. _____
4. Fall is one. _____
5. A single unit. _____
6. Essential. _____
7. A grain. _____
8. A color. _____
9. To be in debt. _____
10. Much money or property. _____
11. An instrument for measuring temperatures. _____
12. A bursting forth or out. _____
13. The smallest of the Great Lakes. _____
14. A state in the Midwest. _____
15. A state on the West Coast. _____

Word Puzzles 31

The following clues help you figure out the five-letter words to which they refer. Start at item 1, and go on changing only one letter in each word to make a new word.

1. You ride in this. _____

2. The part of you that thinks. _____

3. You can do this to your hair. _____

4. You do this to cattle. _____

5. Something mild. _____

6. A hair color. _____

7. The fluid circulating in your body. _____

8. A flower. _____

9. You use this to sweep. _____

10. The husband of the bride. _____

Word Puzzles 32

The following clues help you to figure out the words to which they refer. In each word the last two letters are the reverse of the first two letters. (That is, if the first two letters of the word are ge, the last two letters of the word would have to be eg.)

1. Midday. _____
2. One who likes books. _____
3. To sound or blow a horn. _____
4. To look through a small opening. _____
5. Something that is done. _____
6. Form of address used for a woman. _____
7. Even. _____
8. A device used to catch car speeders. _____
9. A group of something arranged in some order. _____
10. A dog trained to fetch game. _____
11. A belief. _____

Word Puzzles 33

Below are 12 clues for 12 words. Each word starts and ends with the same two letters.

1. You have this when your head hurts. _____
2. The first name of the first president. _____
3. Another way to say, "Hush! Be quiet!" _____
4. A place to worship. _____
5. You use this to remove writing. _____
6. A vegetable with a strong, sharp smell and taste.

   _____

7. A period of ten years. _____
8. Another word for *snapshot* or *picture*. _____
9. To bring to an end. _____
10. Moderate; neither very hot nor very cold (climate).

    _____

11. Another way to say, "Father." _____
12. You are this after a lot of schooling. _____

Word Puzzles 34

Below are 14 clues for 14 words. Each word starts and ends with the same two letters.

1. A vegetable that has a strong, sharp smell and taste. _____ ____

2. Another way of saying, "Mother." _____

3. When a prisoner or animal in a cage gets away. _____

4. Another word for *record player.* _____

5. What you call fish in a hard shell. _____

6. What you call a person on the same team as you. _____

7. Something that removes chalk and pencil marks. _____

8. Submarines use this instrument to look around underwater. _____

9. An object used to stand for something. _____

10. The properties a person leaves in his or her will. _____

11. Any soft-bodied social insect. _____

12. A public speaker. _____

13. Another word for *deceive, trick,* or *make a fool of.* _____

14. To end. _____

Word Puzzles 35

Below are ten clues for ten words. After you guess the first word, the last two letters of each preceding word begin the next word.

1. You write with this. _____
2. This is the opposite of *exit*. _____
3. This gets rid of words. _____
4. This refers to a mistake. _____
5. This is the name of a bird. _____
6. You find these on trees. _____
7. This also means "crucial." _____
8. When friendly countries are bound to your country, you call them this. _____
9. This refers to an approximate amount. _____
10. You find this person in school. _____

Word Puzzles 36

Below are ten clues for ten words. After you guess the first word, the last two letters of each preceding word begin the next word.

1. A sudden rush of air; a violent explosion. _____
2. A piece of rock. _____
3. The opposite of *always*. _____
4. To rub out; to remove all marks of. _____
5. An underground drain used to carry off water and waste matter. _____
6. A mistake. _____
7. A command; a list of things; a proper arrangement of things. _____
8. To become worn away. _____
9. A devil or evil spirit. _____
10. A plant that is eaten that has a strong, sharp smell and taste. _____

Word Puzzles 37

Below are 15 clues to 15 words. Each word has five letters and the middle letter of each word is always the next letter of the alphabet. The first is done for you.

1. A duck makes this sound.   <u>q</u> <u>u</u> a <u>c</u> <u>k</u>
2. This is a strong wire rope.   __ __ b __ __
3. This is something made for speed.   __ __ c __ __
4. This is a snake. (Clue: Think of arithmetic.)   __ __ d __ __
5. The sky is this when it's free from clouds.   __ __ e __ __
6. Long-sleeved shirts have these.   __ __ f __ __
7. This is an instrument used by the military.   __ __ g __ __
8. This is another word for *pains*.   __ __ h __ __
9. A person who can't see is this.   __ __ i __ __
10. An Indian prince or king.   __ __ j __ __
11. This is someone who walks a lot.   __ __ k __ __
12. This refers to a back tooth.   __ __ l __ __
13. This is a desert animal.   __ __ m __ __
14. This is a place where cattle are raised.   __ __ n __ __
15. Football players do this.   __ __ o __ __

Word Puzzles 38

Below are 12 clues for 12 words. Each word has five letters, and the middle letter of each word is always the next letter of the alphabet.

1. To speak with exaggeration about yourself.   __ __ a __ __
2. Work.   __ __ b __ __
3. Referring to a small area or neighborhood.   __ __ c __ __
4. A cabin or cottage.   __ __ d __ __
5. The largest organized unit of naval ships.   __ __ e __ __
6. A thin, crisp cake or biscuit.   __ __ f __ __
7. A brass wind instrument.   __ __ g __ __
8. An anesthetic.   __ __ h __ __
9. A tool that makes holes in firm material.   __ __ i __ __
10. Take pleasure in.   __ __ j __ __
11. Part of the leg.   __ __ k __ __
12. A tooth.   __ __ l __ __

Word Puzzles 39

Below are clues to eight words. Each new word adds one letter and uses all the letters of the word preceding it. To form the new word you can rearrange the letters in any way you wish. The first is done for you.

1. An indefinite article.   <u>a</u>
2. Another way of saying, "Father." (two letters)   _____
3. A health resort. (three letters)   _____
4. A fight. (four letters)   _____
5. Holds things together. (five letters)   _____
6. A meal. (six letters)   _____
7. To say again. (seven letters)   _____
8. To set apart. (eight letters)   _____

Word Puzzles 40

Below are 14 clues to 14 words. Each word has five letters, and the middle letter of each word is always the next letter of the alphabet.

1. A means of transportation.   _ _ a _ _
2. A bird.   _ _ b _ _
3. Your mother's brother.   _ _ c _ _
4. A snake.   _ _ d _ _
5. Comes from a cow.   _ _ e _ _
6. A weapon.   _ _ f _ _
7. A prejudiced person.   _ _ g _ _
8. What is left after being burned.   _ _ h _ _
9. A vegetable with a strong, sharp taste.   _ _ i _ _
10. A prince in India.   _ _ j _ _
11. One who walks a lot.   _ _ k _ _
12. Red is one.   _ _ l _ _
13. An illness.   _ _ m _ _
14. A boat with light paddles.   _ _ n _ _

Word Puzzles 41

The following clues help you figure out the words to which they refer. In each word the last two letters are the reverse of the first two letters. Examples: noon, deed, radar.

1. A girl's name. _____
2. One who likes books. _____
3. Means the same as *devout* or *affectionate*. _____
4. Looks over carefully. _____
5. The ways people behave socially. _____

Word Puzzles 42

The following clues help you figure out the five-letter words to which they refer. Start at item 1, and go on changing only one letter in each word to make a new word that fits the clue.

1. A practical joke. _____
2. A grouch. _____
3. To break. _____
4. Trail. _____
5. Evidence of some past thing. _____
6. Something that connects. _____
7. Courageous. _____

Word Puzzles 43

Below are ten clues to ten words. Each word has one more letter than the preceding word, and the last letter of the preceding word begins the next word.

1. Opposite of *yes*.   _____
2. A nocturnal bird.   _____
3. Opposite of *first*.   _____
4. A wild animal.   _____
5. Used in tennis.   _____
6. House on wheels.   _____
7. To have set free.   _____
8. To remove water from.   _____
9. Coming to an end.   _____
10. Your origin.   _____

Word Puzzles 44

Following are clues for seven words. Although the clue for each word is different, the words all share a common meaning. (Hint: something supernatural.)

1. A faint, shadowy trace. _____
2. An unusual or unexpected sight. _____
3. A special attitude or frame of mind. _____
4. Something seen. _____
5. One that has unusual drive. _____
6. Something existing in appearance only. _____
7. Something that haunts the mind. _____

Word Square Puzzle 45

Below is a Hunting Square. If you follow the directions carefully, you will track down the animal that escaped from the zoo.

```
A  F  A  R  M  S
P  L  G  O  G  R
S  T  R  E  E  T
S  T  O  P  I  T
R  O  C  D  I  P
B  A  K  E  S  C
```

Directions: *(1) Each clue, hidden in the square, helps you find a letter. Read each carefully. (2) Put the letters together to hunt down the animal.*

Clues:

1. Go to the end of the *street.* _____
2. Look in the center of *pit.* _____
3. Look at the top of *rock.* _____
4. Look at the end of *tree.* _____
5. Look in the middle of *farms.* _____

_____

Word Square Puzzle 46

Below is a mystery Treasure Square Hunt. If you follow directions carefully, you will track down the mystery treasure.

```
H   A   J   P   A   P
I   V   D   I   S   O
L   E   I   E   U   L
L   N   G   R   N   I
Y   U   P   U   B   C
B   E   A   R   S   E
```

Directions: *(1) Each clue hidden in the square helps you to find a letter. Read each clue carefully. (2) Put the letters together to find the mystery treasure.*

Clues:

1. Start with the tenth letter of the alphabet, and go two letters to the left. _____

2. Go to the end of the *avenue*, and turn right one letter. _____

3. Go to the top of *hill*, and turn five letters to the right. _____

4. Find another word for *father*. Take the beginning letter.

   _____

5. Find the word that tells you what you do with a shovel. Take its middle letter. _____

6. Go to the end of *pier*. Move one letter to the right so that you won't fall into the water. _____

7. Do you see the escaped bears? If you do, do not go near them. Quickly run for help. Find persons who can help you. Take their last letter.

   _____

8. You can help by carefully going near the bears and taking away the letter that makes things increase. _____

9. If you find the word that makes things bright and take the first letter, you've completed your Treasure Square Hunt. _____

   _____

Word Square Puzzle 47

Below is a Word Square containing 60 words of two or more letters. You can go across and down to find them. Some words appear more than once and in the plural, but they still count!

```
S  O  R  E  A  D  D
H  A  I  R  Y  E  T
E  R  N  E  S  T  O
L  I  D  S  O  O  N
F  O  O  T  N  U  T
O  R  E  A  L  R  O
R  E  A  Y  E  S  E
```

Across

1. _____   16. _____
2. _____   17. _____
3. _____   18. _____
4. _____   19. _____
5. _____   20. _____
6. _____   21. _____
7. _____   22. _____
8. _____   23. _____
9. _____   24. _____
10. _____   25. _____
11. _____   26. _____
12. _____   27. _____
13. _____   28. _____
14. _____   29. _____
15. _____

Down

1. _____   17. _____
2. _____   18. _____
3. _____   19. _____
4. _____   20. _____
5. _____   21. _____
6. _____   22. _____
7. _____   23. _____
8. _____   24. _____
9. _____   25. _____
10. _____   26. _____
11. _____   27. _____
12. _____   28. _____
13. _____   29. _____
14. _____   30. _____
15. _____   31. _____
16. _____   32. _____

Word Square Puzzle 48

Below is a word square containing 131 words of two or more letters. You can go across and down to find them. Some words appear more than once, but they still count! (One word is a contraction.)

```
S  C  E  N  T  E  R  R  O  R
C  A  P  E  A  R  E  E  L  M
O  R  I  A  N  O  M  A  D  E
R  R  C  R  Y  D  I  D  E  N
E  Y  E  A  R  E  N  T  O  D
D  R  I  P  E  N  D  I  N  E
P  A  L  P  I  T  Y  E  S  E
A  T  L  O  N  L  Y  E  A  R
D  O  O  R  A  N  G  E  T  I
N  O  B  T  P  O  O  R  E  E
```

Across

1. _____   18. _____   36. _____   54. _____
2. _____   19. _____   37. _____   55. _____
3. _____   20. _____   38. _____   56. _____
4. _____   21. _____   39. _____   57. _____
5. _____   22. _____   40. _____   58. _____
6. _____   23. _____   41. _____   59. _____
7. _____   24. _____   42. _____   60. _____
8. _____   25. _____   43. _____   61. _____
9. _____   26. _____   44. _____   62. _____
10. _____   27. _____   45. _____   63. _____
11. _____   28. _____   46. _____   64. _____
12. _____   29. _____   47. _____   65. _____
13. _____   30. _____   48. _____   66. _____
14. _____   31. _____   49. _____   67. _____
15. _____   32. _____   50. _____   68. _____
16. _____   33. _____   51. _____   69. _____
17. _____   34. _____   52. _____   70. _____
                    35. _____   53. _____   71. _____

Name _____ Class _____ Date _____

Down

1. _____	16. _____	31. _____	46. _____
2. _____	17. _____	32. _____	47. _____
3. _____	18. _____	33. _____	48. _____
4. _____	19. _____	34. _____	49. _____
5. _____	20. _____	35. _____	50. _____
6. _____	21. _____	36. _____	51. _____
7. _____	22. _____	37. _____	52. _____
8. _____	23. _____	38. _____	53. _____
9. _____	24. _____	39. _____	54. _____
10. _____	25. _____	40. _____	55. _____
11. _____	26. _____	41. _____	56. _____
12. _____	27. _____	42. _____	57. _____
13. _____	28. _____	43. _____	58. _____
14. _____	29. _____	44. _____	59. _____
15. _____	30. _____	45. _____	60. _____

Word Square Puzzle 49

Below is a word square containing 23 water creatures. You can go across and down to find them. See how many you can find.

```
S  A  L  M  O  N  A  C  M  T  A
Q  P  E  R  C  H  S  L  U  S  L
U  O  E  H  T  U  N  A  S  C  H
I  S  L  C  O  D  A  M  S  A  A
D  P  O  R  P  O  I  S  E  L  D
W  E  R  A  U  Y  L  H  L  L  D
H  A  B  B  S  S  E  A  L  O  O
A  L  O  B  S  T  E  R  E  P  C
L  E  H  A  K  E  K  K  E  I  K
E  L  H  E  R  R  I  N  G  K  R
A  H  A  L  I  B  U  T  O  E  L
```

Across		Down	
1. _____	6. _____	1. _____	8. _____
2. _____	7. _____	2. _____	9. _____
3. _____	8. _____	3. _____	10. _____
4. _____	9. _____	4. _____	11. _____
5. _____	10. _____	5. _____	12. _____
		6. _____	13. _____
		7. _____	

Word Square Puzzle 50

Below is a word square containing 36 plants, including flowers and trees. You can go across and down to find them.

```
F E R N B E G O N I A G T I C
C A L M O N D E E T U L I P L
H B I O M A P L E B O A R O O
R L P A P A L M M E I D I P U
Y U A L E V I O L E T I S L D
S E C S T O L A I C A O E A B
A B H N U C Y K L H S L R R E
N E Y A N A O C A C T U S O R
T L S P I D A E C P E S I P R
H L A D A O R O S E R E A I Y
E Z N R B C A R N A T I O N A
M E D A I S Y C O R O M E E S
U B R G A E O H Y A C I N T H
M R A O N I B I R C H I V E E
O A R N D A N D E L I O N R O
```

	Across			Down	
1. ____	9. ____		1. ____	12. ____	
2. ____	10. ____		2. ____	13. ____	
3. ____	11. ____		3. ____	14. ____	
4. ____	12. ____		4. ____	15. ____	
5. ____	13. ____		5. ____	16. ____	
6. ____	14. ____		6. ____	17. ____	
7. ____	15. ____		7. ____	18. ____	
8. ____			8. ____	19. ____	
			9. ____	20. ____	
			10. ____	21. ____	
			11. ____		

221

Word Square Puzzle 51

There are 25 words in the word square that have to do with banks and banking. You can go across and down to find them. See how many you can find.

```
A  G  O  V  E  R  D  R  A  W  N  O  C
S  O  B  B  O  L  D  R  A  F  T  S  R
U  L  O  A  N  I  S  D  T  U  A  P  E
M  O  R  T  G  A  G  E  C  A  S  O  D
O  S  R  K  R  B  L  B  H  R  S  S  I
N  T  O  E  C  I  N  T  E  R  E  S  T
E  A  W  X  A  L  A  N  C  E  T  A  O
Y  N  E  C  S  I  A  N  K  A  F  V  R
B  D  R  H  H  T  P  U  B  R  D  I  W
O  A  N  A  L  Y  R  V  O  S  I  N  R
N  R  O  N  B  A  N  K  O  E  C  G  S
D  D  O  G  O  L  D  R  K  L  M  S  A
S  E  D  E  P  O  S  I  T  I  M  E  O
```

Across

1. _____   5. _____
2. _____   6. _____
3. _____   7. _____
4. _____

Down

1. _____   10. _____
2. _____   11. _____
3. _____   12. _____
4. _____   13. _____
5. _____   14. _____
6. _____   15. _____
7. _____   16. _____
8. _____   17. _____
9. _____   18. _____

Word Square Puzzle 52

Below is a word square containing 59 words of two or more letters. You can go across and down to find them. Some words appear more than once, but they still count!

```
T  E  A  C  H  E  R
H  O  L  D  A  L  E
E  N  T  E  R  H  A
A  E  A  B  E  E  L
T  W  R  I  T  E  T
E  E  E  T  E  L  O
R  I  D  E  A  L  R
```

Across

1. _____ 14. _____
2. _____ 15. _____
3. _____ 16. _____
4. _____ 17. _____
5. _____ 18. _____
6. _____ 19. _____
7. _____ 20. _____
8. _____ 21. _____
9. _____ 22. _____
10. _____ 23. _____
11. _____ 24. _____
12. _____ 25. _____
13. _____

Down

1. _____ 18. _____
2. _____ 19. _____
3. _____ 20. _____
4. _____ 21. _____
5. _____ 22. _____
6. _____ 23. _____
7. _____ 24. _____
8. _____ 25. _____
9. _____ 26. _____
10. _____ 27. _____
11. _____ 28. _____
12. _____ 29. _____
13. _____ 30. _____
14. _____ 31. _____
15. _____ 32. _____
16. _____ 33. _____
17. _____ 34. _____

Word Square Puzzle 53

There are 18 words in the mystery Word Square that are similar in meaning to the word in the vertical center of the square. You can go across and down to find them.

```
A  D  S  B  R  I  G  H  T  E  R
R  E  H  R  K  N  O  W  I  N  G
T  X  R  I  S  T  E  E  R  S  P
S  T  E  L  K  E  E  N  O  M  R
A  E  W  L  A  L  E  R  T  A  U
P  R  D  I  C  L  E  V  E  R  D
I  O  E  A  W  I  S  E  O  T  E
E  U  F  N  I  G  S  A  G  E  N
N  S  T  T  L  E  X  P  E  R  T
T  I  N  G  E  N  I  O  U  S  T
A  D  R  O  I  T  S  H  A  R  P
```

Across

1. _____ 7. _____
2. _____ 8. _____
3. _____ 9. _____
4. _____ 10. _____
5. _____ 11. _____
6. _____

Down

1. _____ 5. _____
2. _____ 6. _____
3. _____ 7. _____
4. _____

Word Rectangle Puzzle 54

In the following word rectangle there are 49 animals, including birds, fish, and snakes. You can go across or down to find them. See how many you can find.

```
R C A T T P I G H A M S T E R A L S L
H S P I D E R O O S T E R A B B I T A
I A E H O G D O R P E A C O C K O E M
N L N S M O O S E E E L E P H A N T B
O M G H T I G E R O K F A H O R S E S
C O U E B O A R A M C O W O R M F C H
E N I E A G L E T E R X A L N A L R A
R A N P T O A D S W A N S B E E Y O R
O O G I R A F F E A B A P O T L T W K
S F R O G T U R K E Y O C E L O T A S
```

Across		Down	
1. _____	15. _____	1. _____	12. _____
2. _____	16. _____	2. _____	13. _____
3. _____	17. _____	3. _____	14. _____
4. _____	18. _____	4. _____	15. _____
5. _____	19. _____	5. _____	16. _____
6. _____	20. _____	6. _____	17. _____
7. _____	21. _____	7. _____	18. _____
8. _____	22. _____	8. _____	19. _____
9. _____	23. _____	9. _____	20. _____
10. _____	24. _____	10. _____	21. _____
11. _____	25. _____	11. _____	22. _____
12. _____	26. _____		
13. _____	27. _____		
14. _____			

Word Rectangle Puzzle 55

In the following word rectangle there are 36 things that you can find in a house. You can find the words by going across and down. See how good you are in finding them.

```
C D M P E O P L E O R D O O R S C S
L R I L O L K I T C H E N D U A O R
O A R A B A F L O O R S T E G W U A
S P R N E M S H E E T S A N B I C D
E E O T D P T E L E V I S I O N H I
T S R S R S O F A F A N F O O D A O
S P S P O T S C L O C K T V K O I D
N E S T O V E N P I L L O W S W R E
R T L A M P I C T U R E S T E P S S
E S C O T R E F R I G E R A T O R K
```

Across

1. _____
2. _____
3. _____
4. _____
5. _____
6. _____
7. _____
8. _____
9. _____
10. _____
11. _____
12. _____
13. _____
14. _____
15. _____
16. _____
17. _____
18. _____
19. _____

Down

1. _____
2. _____
3. _____
4. _____
5. _____
6. _____
7. _____
8. _____
9. _____
10. _____
11. _____
12. _____
13. _____
14. _____
15. _____
16. _____
17. _____

Word Riddle Puzzle 56

I used to be but exist no more,
I could walk on two or four.
Who or what am I?
D _ _ _ _ _ _ _

***The answer to this riddle is an eight-letter word made up
of the letters that are left over from the word riddles below.
The first is done for you.***

1. I mean "fear" (dread), but when you take away my first letter, I'm
   what you do to a book (read). The left over letter is *d*. _____d_____

2. I mean "perfect," but when you take away my first letter, I'm what you
   do to cards. _____

3. I mean "small in width," but when you take away my first letter, I am
   something that points the way. _____

4. I am a fruit, but when you take away my first letter, I'm something you
   can cook on. _____

5. I'm what's left from a wound, but when you take away my first letter,
   you can drive in me. _____

6. I am the smallest particle of an element, but when you take away my
   first letter, I become a boy's name. _____

7. I am any fixed quanity, but when you take away my first letter, I
   become the egg of an insect. _____

8. I'm a running contest, but when you take away my first letter, I
   become the highest and lowest card in a deck. _____

_____

Word Riddle Puzzle 57

What has a bed but never sleeps? Each sentence below gives you a clue to a letter. When you put the letters together, you will have the answer to the riddle.

_____ 1. My first letter is in *tired,* but not in *diets.*

_____ 2. My second letter is in *relieve,* but not in *lever.*

_____ 3. My third letter is in *driver,* but not in *drearier.*

_____ 4. My fourth letter is in *primer,* but not in *primary.*

_____ 5. My fifth letter is in *shriek,* but not in *sheik.*

_____

Word Riddle Puzzle 58

Each sentence below gives you a clue to a letter. When you put the letters together, you will have the answer to this riddle: "What grows shorter, the longer it stands?"

_____ 1. The first letter is in *mice*, but not in *mine*.

_____ 2. The second letter is in *train*, but not in *trinket*.

_____ 3. The third letter is in *cone*, but not in *come*.

_____ 4. The fourth letter is in *read*, but not in *rear*.

_____ 5. The fifth letter is in *mile*, but not in *mine*.

_____ 6. The sixth letter is in *reason*, but not in ransom.

_____

Word Riddle Puzzle 59

Each sentence below gives you a clue to a letter. When you put the letters together, you will have the answer to this riddle: "What is not clothing but worn by feet?

_____ 1. My first letter is in *searched*, but not in *shared*.

_____ 2. My second letter is in *stream*, but not in *meters*.

_____ 3. My third letter is in *bearer*, but not in *beast*.

_____ 4. My fourth letter is in *drapery*, but not in *dreary*.

_____ 5. My fifth letter is in *trickery*, but not in *tricky*.

_____ 6. My sixth letter is in *consent*, but not in *console*.

_____

Word Riddle Puzzle 60

Each sentence below gives you a clue to a letter. When you put the letters together, you will have the answer to this riddle: "What toe never wears a shoe?"

_____ 1. Its first letter is in *dream*, but not in *dread*.

_____ 2. Its second letter is in *smile*, but not in *smell*.

_____ 3. Its third letter is in *castle*, but not in *cattle*.

_____ 4. Its fourth letter is in *bought*, but not in *bough*.

_____ 5. Its fifth letter is in *settle*, but not in *stare*.

_____ 6. Its sixth letter is in *wreath*, but not in *wrath*.

_____ 7. Its seventh letter is in *dessert*, but not in *deserve*.

_____ 8. Its eighth letter is in *rode*, but not in *read*.

_____ 9. Its ninth letter is in *please*, but not in *plastic*.

_____

Word Riddle Puzzle 61

Each sentence below gives you a clue to a letter. When you put the letters together, you will have the answer to this riddle: "What small thing never runs out of light in the night?"

_____ 1. Its first letter is in *calf*, but not in *calm*.

_____ 2. Its second letter is in *nine*, but not in *neat*.

_____ 3. Its third letter is in *trays*, but not in *tasty*.

_____ 4. Its fourth letter is in *bean*, but not in *band*.

_____ 5. Its fifth letter is in *after*, but not in *alter*.

_____ 6. Its sixth letter is in *place*, but not in *peace*.

_____ 7. Its seventh letter is in *pray*, but not in *rapid*.

_____

Word Riddle Puzzle 62

After a big feast, I go for a very big sleep. What or who am I? Each sentence below gives you a clue to a letter. When you put the letters together, you will have the answer to the riddle.

_____ 1. My first letter is in *match*, but not in *hamster*.
_____ 2. My second letter is in *clean*, but not in *clench*.
_____ 3. My third letter is in *polite*, but not in *police*.
_____ 4. My fourth letter is in *smear*, but not in *smart*.
_____ 5. My fifth letter is in *brain*, but not in *cabin*.
_____ 6. My sixth letter is in *cape*, but not in *care*.
_____ 7. My seventh letter is in *mine*, but not in *mean*.
_____ 8. My eighth letter is in *salad*, but not in *sadder*.
_____ 9. My ninth letter is in *almond*, but not in *Monday*.
_____ 10. My tenth letter is in *beach*, but not in *bench*.
_____ 11. My eleventh letter is in *train*, but not in *stain*.

_____

Word Riddle Puzzle 63

What keeps things out and runs around the yard, yet never moves? Each sentence below gives you a clue to a letter. When you put the letters together, you will have the answer to the riddle.

_____ 1. My first letter is in *safe*, but not in *save*.

_____ 2. My second letter is in *search*, but not in *starch*.

_____ 3. My third letter is in *grand*, but not in *grade*.

_____ 4. My fourth letter is in *place*, but not in *plane*.

_____ 5. My fifth letter is in *pearl*, but not in *parlor*.

_____

Word Riddle Puzzle 64

What stays hot even when it's cold? Each of the following sentences gives you a clue to a letter. When you put the letters together, you will have the answer to the riddle.

_____ 1. The first letter is in *special*, but not in *sociable*.

_____ 2. The second letter is in *beast*, but not in *blast*.

_____ 3. The third letter is in *spider*, but not in *slider*.

_____ 4. The fourth letter is in *depose*, but not in *diagnose*.

_____ 5. The fifth letter is in *reader*, but not in *radar*.

_____ 6. The sixth letter is in *print*, but not in *paint*.

_____

Word Riddle Puzzle 65

A child is lost. You can help. Each sentence below gives you a clue to a letter. When you put the letters together, you will know where the child is.

_____ 1. My first letter is in *east*, but not in *west*.

_____ 2. My second letter is in *west*, but not in *swell*.

_____ 3. My third letter is in *batch*, but not in *bachelor*.

_____ 4. My fourth letter is in *father*, but not in *falter*.

_____ 5. My fifth letter is in *bathe*, but not in *bath*.

_____ 6. My sixth letter is in *zebra*, but not in *break*.

_____ 7. My seventh letter is in *groom*, but not in *grumble*.

_____ 8. My eighth letter is in *broad*, but not in *bread*.

_____

Rhyming Word Puzzles 66

The following clues help you figure out the words to which they refer. Hint: All the words rhyme.

1. Someone who doesn't tell the truth. _____

2. It burns. _____

3. A car needs this. _____

4. Opposite of lower. _____

5. A long, thin thread of metal. _____

6. Wet clothes go in this. _____

7. A tender young chicken. _____

8. A group of singers. _____

9. To get the services of. _____

10. Deep mud. _____

11. Male parent of four-legged animals. _____

12. Terrible. _____

Rhyming Word Puzzles 67

The following clues help you figure out the words to which they refer. Hint: All the words rhyme.

1. A number.   _____
2. A tree.   _____
3. A hog.   _____
4. Belonging to me.   _____
5. Something to drink.   _____
6. To glow with light.   _____
7. Money you pay as a penalty.   _____
8. To take any meal.   _____
9. A strong thread or string.   _____
10. A long, thin mark.   _____
11. An indication.   _____
12. A river flowing through West Germany. _____
13. Salt water.   _____
14. A long, slender stem that creeps
    on the ground.   _____

Rhyming Word Puzzles 68

The following clues help you figure out the words to which they refer. Hint: All the words rhyme.

1. A fight. _____
2. A highway. _____
3. Uncertainty. _____
4. A prolonged period of dryness. _____
5. To sulk. _____
6. An oaf (big, clumsy slow-witted person). _____
7. An illness. _____

Rhyming Word Puzzles 69

The answers for each of the following clues are two *rhyming words.*

1. Mean boy. _____ _____
2. Ridiculous horse. _____ _____
3. Kitchen knife. _____ _____
4. Window cover. _____ _____
5. Funny folklore character. _____ _____

Rhyming Word Puzzles 70

The answers for each of the following clues are two *rhyming words.*

1. Obese rodent. _____ _____
2. Weak boy. _____ _____
3. Underdone rabbit. _____ _____
4. Crazy villain. _____ _____
5. An unruly young person. _____ _____
6. Wheel guard indentation. _____ _____

Rhyming Word Puzzles 71

The answers for each of the following clues are two rhyming words.

1. Amusing rabbit. _____ _____
2. Librarian's enemy. _____ _____
3. Noisy mob. _____ _____
4. Equal amount. _____ _____
5. Angry, tiresome person. _____ _____

Rhyming Word Puzzles 72

The answers for each of the following clues are two
rhyming words.

1. Moist animal. _____ _____
2. Girl friend. _____ _____
3. Considerable bet. _____ _____
4. Subdued amusement. _____ _____
5. Animal offspring. _____ _____
6. Exhausted fish. _____ _____

Scrambled Word Puzzles 73

Name _____ Class _____ Date _____

Two words are combined to make a scrambled set. The letters for each word in the scrambled set are presented in order, *but the two words are mixed together. A clue is given for each set. The first is done for you.*

1. Two farm animals.   gocoawt   goat   cow
2. Two colors.   pruerpdle   _____   _____
3. Two flowers.   draiossey   _____   _____
4. Two fruits.   pgreaapceh   _____   _____
5. Two insects.   awanstp   _____   _____
6. Two vegetables.   bepeana   _____   _____
7. Two wild animals.   tibegaerr   _____   _____
8. Two trees.   pmianpele   _____   _____
9. Two birds.   clanarakry   _____   _____
10. Two seafoods.   foloyunstdeerr _____   _____

244

Scrambled Word Puzzles 74

Two words are combined to make a scrambled set. The letters for each word in the scrambled set are presented in order, but the two words are mixed together. A clue is given for each set.

1. Domestic animals. cdaotg _____ _____
2. Birds. priogeboinn _____ _____
3. Wild animals. wgoolrilfla _____ _____
4. Eight-legged creatures. stpiicdekr _____ _____
5. Flowers. tviuolliept _____ _____
6. Trees. wmialplloew _____ _____
7. Fish. tcrooudt _____ _____
8. Fruits. paipnpealpeple _____ _____

Scrambled Word Puzzles 75

Rearrange the letters of each word so that they fit the given clue for a new word.

1. Pan: something you take when you're tired. _____
2. Now: the opposite of *lost*. _____
3. Net: the number of dimes in a dollar. _____
4. Seat: a direction. _____
5. Late: a story. _____
6. Name: a horse has this. _____
7. Rat: a thick, sticky black liquid. _____
8. Car: a bowlike curved line. _____
9. More: an Italian city. _____
10. Near: to attain or gain. _____
11. Able: a large package. _____
12. Rope: a tiny opening in skin. _____
13. Pear: to cut down a harvest. _____
14. Pane: the back of the neck. _____
15. Nab: to prohibit. _____

Scrambled Word Puzzles 76

Rearrange the letters of each word so that they fit the given clues for a new word.

1. Was: something to cut with. _____
2. Sale: an emblem; a sea mammal. _____
3. Lump: a fruit. _____
4. Deal: to show the way; to begin; a heavy, soft, bluish-gray metallic chemical. _____
5. Slap: a dog does this to liquid with its tongue. _____
6. Line: I'm the name of the longest river in Africa. _____
7. Life: an orderly arrangement of cards, papers, and so on.

   _____
8. Cents: an odor. _____
9. Wears: to pledge or vow an oath. _____
10. Live: wicked; worthless. _____

Scrambled Word Puzzles 77

Below are incomplete scrambled words and a clue for each one. Add one letter to the incomplete scrambled word to get the correct answer. The first one is done for you.

1. iks—not well _____ sick _____
2. ule—a color _____
3. eim—a coin _____
4. kli—something to drink _____
5. lai—it comes from the sky _____
6. nas—found at the beach _____
7. ram—a female horse _____
8. nak—money is kept here _____
9. soe—a flower _____
10. ria—a place that has lots of rides _____
11. yra—you carry things on this _____
12. veo—a bird _____
13. aie— one who helps _____
14. iec—a grain _____
15. psa—a flying insect _____

Scrambled Word Puzzles 78

Below are a word, a letter, and a clue. Put the word and letter together, and you have the answer to the clue. (To get the answer, you can rearrange the letters in any way.)

1. Cow plus *r* equals a bird. _____
2. Saw plus *p* equals an insect. _____
3. Low plus *f* equals a wild animal. _____
4. Nut plus *a* equals a fish. _____
5. Rue plus *p* equals a country. _____

Scrambled Word Puzzles 79

Below are a word, a letter, and a clue. Put the word and letter together, and you have the answer to the clue. (To get the answer, you can rearrange the letters in any way.)

1. Sat plus *e* equals a direction. _____
2. Lap plus *i* equals a container. _____
3. Sea plus *e* equals freedom from care. _____
4. Are plus *r* equals the back part of something. _____
5. Hoe plus *c* equals the repetition of a sound. _____
6. Kin plus *m* equals soft fur. _____
7. Fee plus *r* equals a chain of rocks at or near the surface of the water.

_____

Scrambled Word Puzzles 80

Below are a word, two letters, and a clue. Put the word and letters together, and you have the answer to the clue. (To get the answer, you can rearrange the letters in any way.)

1. Seal plus *e* and *p* equals a polite word. _____

2. Sire plus *t* and *p* equals a clergyman. _____

3. Maine plus *r* and *r* equals a seaman. _____

4. Acre plus *d* and *s* equals something holy. _____

5. Ale plus *g* and *l* equals something lawful. _____

6. Dig plus *e* and *r* equals a range of hills or mountains. _____

7. Died plus *i* and *v* equals "to separate." _____

Scrambled Word Puzzles 81

Two words are combined to make a scrambled set. The letters for each word in the scrambled set are presented in order, but the two words are mixed together. A clue is given for each set.

1. Amphibians (land
   and water animals). tforaodg   _____ _____
2. Mollusks (shellfish). omuysssetelr _____ _____
3. Spices.   npuetpmpeegr _____ _____
4. Plants.   maollgade   _____ _____
5. Birds.   lhoaownk   _____ _____
6. Reptiles.   scnrocaokdiele _____ _____
7. Pachyderms
   (thick-skinned).   rehliepnhoacnerots _____ _____

Scrambled Word Puzzles 82

Below are a word, a letter, and a clue. Put the word and letter together, and you have the answer to the clue. (To get the answer, you can rearrange the letters in any way.)

1. Raid plus *y* equals a place where butter or cheese is made.
   _____

2. And plus *k* equals unpleasantly moist. _____

3. Liar plus *t* equals a tryout. _____

4. New plus *a* equals decline. _____

5. Nice plus *w* equals flinch. _____

6. Red plus *u* equals coarse. _____

7. Rode plus *r* equals command. _____

Scrambled Word Puzzles 83

Below are a word, two letters, and a clue. Put the word and letters together, and you have the answer to the clue. (To get the answer, you can rearrange the letters in any way.)

1. Team plus *r* and *s* equals a body of running water. _____
2. Nice plus *o* and *t* equals a written announcement. _____
3. Leer plus *a* and *v* equals "to make known." _____
4. Lame plus *i* and *c* equals ill will. _____
5. Cane plus *p* and *r* equals how a horse moves. _____
6. Rain plus *c* and *d* equals spoiled. _____

Scrambled Word Puzzles 84

After you unscramble the letters below, you will find 13 words that have the same meaning. Hint: Each word refers to a person who is not easily frightened, and the first letter of each word is underlined. (You can use the dictionary to help you.)

1. ea_b_vr _____
2. rea_f_ssel _____
3. l_d_bo _____
4. reag_c_uoosu _____
5. n_u_arfiad _____
6. ra_d_gni _____
7. yc_k_pul _____
8. inatla_v_ _____
9. lla_g_nat _____
10. n_u_udanedt _____
11. n_t_ipedri _____
12. n_u_ntiiimatedd _____
13. ssel_d_uant _____

Hidden Word Puzzles 85

Find what is hidden in each of the sentences. The words
in the parentheses will tell you what to look for. Hint: The
answer may be hidden in one or more words of the sentence.
The first one is done for you.

1. Little Red Riding Hood wore a red cape. (an animal) ____(c)ape____
2. My father has a beard. (an animal) _____
3. I am a catcher in baseball. (an animal) _____
4. My mother has a very pretty pearl necklace. (a fruit) _____
5. I don't like to peel potatoes. (a fish) _____
6. It's not good to cram for exams. (an animal) _____
7. The children laughed whenever the funny camel Liar told lies in the fairy tale. (a flower) _____
8. I have a high yen and hope that you will remain with us. (an animal) _____
9. My father says that your prestige remains if you continue to achieve. (an animal) _____
10. Some people have very low aspirations. (an insect and a snake) _____

Hidden Word Puzzles 86

*Find what is hidden in each of the sentences. The words
in the parentheses will tell you what to look for. Hint: The
answer may be hidden in one or more words of the sentence.*

1. No one was hurt when the bottle cap exploded. (a wild animal)
   _____

2. The burro seemed to sense that something was wrong. (a flower)
   _____

3. I have a Siamese cat that is very special to me. (a continent)
   _____

4. In the story the thief Al confessed to the crime. (a bird) _____

5. We laughed when my brother Tom, at our party, played the role of a
   clown. (a food) _____

6. It's not advisable to buff a long marble floor on your hands and knees.
   (a city) _____

7. We edited the manuscript very carefully. (a plant) _____

8. A dam should be built in that area to control the floods. (a president)
   _____

Hidden Word Puzzles 87

Find what is hidden in each of the sentences. The words in the parentheses will tell you what to look for. Hint: The answer may be hidden in one or more words of the sentence.

1. Mother Goose rhymes were first published in London about 1760. (an insect) _____

2. Grandma Pleasant is what we call my grandmother. (a tree)
   _____

3. The sea story that the teacher was reading to her class was very exciting. (a direction) _____

4. Neither the devil nor angel can change my friend's mind once he has made it up. (a fruit) _____

5. "Put the pan there," said the cook to his helper. (a wild animal)
   _____

Hidden Word Puzzles 88

Find the name of the state that is hidden in each sentence.
Hint: The answer may be hidden in one or more words of
the sentence. The first is done for you.

1. Washing tons of clothes is not my idea of fun.

   _____

2. The main event will take place tomorrow. _____

3. When we visited India, Nancy became very ill.

   _____

4. A house in the mountains may be nice, but a house near the ocean is
   what I want. _____

5. "Did your brother Al ask a friend to spend the night?" asked my
   mother. _____

6. My sheets have a florid animal pattern on them.

   _____

7. Although many persons have never gone to a foreign land, more go
   now than years before. _____

Hidden Word Puzzles 89

Find the name of the bird *that is hidden in each sentence.*
Hint: The answer may be hidden in one or more words of
the sentence.

1. The dog that I own is a beagle. _____
2. Dick Clark is a singer. _____
3. Now, let's go to the movies. _____
4. Then we went to the baseball game. _____
5. We saw a crab at the fish store. _____
6. My best friend's name is Shaw King. _____
7. The fairy's wand that was used in the play belongs to me.

_____

8. I have a throb in my head. _____
9. The birthday card in Alan's hand is for you. _____
10. We put her on the swing. _____

Hidden Word Puzzles 90

Find the name of the country that is hidden in each sentence. Hint: The name may be hidden in one or more words of the sentence.

1. I went to a lovely spa in the country last week. _____
2. The little boy said, "I am Eric, a good little boy." _____
3. Can a dark window shade keep out the light? _____
4. In his father's den Mark does all of his homework. _____
5. When the shark's fin landed on the boat, we all screamed with fear.

   _____
6. The football hit Al yesterday on his nose. _____
7. His chin and jaw were also hurt. _____
8. Often glands do not function properly. _____
9. In the monster movie, a tigerman yelled and screamed.

   _____
10. The dice landed on the floor rather than on the table. _____

Hidden Clue Puzzles 91

Below are a number of scrambled words with clues for each word. Each unscrambled word has an in it. The first is done for you.

1. You clap with these.   snadh   _____hands_____

2. You use this when you have a cold.   raeichfnhedk   _____

3. Something sweet that tastes good.   ncayd   _____

4. Refers to earth.   anld   _____

5. You use this to cover a part of you that is hurt.   gaendba   _____

6. You keep money in this place.   bkna   _____

7. A loud noise.   ngab   _____

8. Something that grows and has leaves.   ptnal   _____

9. This can fly.   prlneaia   _____

10. When you move about.   rendaw   _____

11. When you are a helper.   ntsastsia   _____

12. This moves around the sun.   aetnlp   _____

Hidden Clue Puzzles 92

Below are 15 clues for 15 words. Hint: Each word has ate *in it.*

1. The opposite of *love*. _____
2. Something you eat from. _____
3. A companion. _____
4. The opposite of *early*. _____
5. Something that swings on hinges and controls entrance.

   _____

6. A sweet fruit. _____
7. California is one. _____
8. To produce. _____
9. To act the same as. _____
10. A large residence. _____
11. To collapse by letting out air. _____
12. To begin. _____
13. To set apart. _____
14. To determine roughly. _____
15. To show the working of. _____

Hidden Clue Puzzles 93

Below are 20 clues for 20 words. Hint: Each word has ant *in it.*

1. An insect. _____
2. You wear these. _____
3. These have flowers and leaves. _____
4. A newborn baby. _____
5. A large animal with a very long nose. _____
6. A ruler with absolute power. _____
7. When you are a helper to someone. _____
8. Sweet-smelling; smells nice. _____
9. Cheerful; agreeable. _____
10. Unreal; purely imaginary. _____
11. Refers to singing. _____
12. At an incline. _____
13. Attached to a television set. _____
14. An animal with horns. _____
15. A fit of bad temper. _____
16. A transparent case enclosing a light. _____
17. When you are in need. _____
18. A former president. _____
19. Brave and noble. _____
20. Not showing interest. _____

Hidden Clue Puzzles 94

Below are ten clues for ten words. Hint: Each word has age in it.

1. You keep an animal in this. _____
2. You find this in a book. _____
3. You earn these. _____
4. You keep a car in here. _____
5. You carry your clothes in this. _____
6. You do this when you direct affairs. _____
7. This refers to how you walk. _____
8. You are in this state if you are violently angry. _____
9. This refers to a wise man. _____
10. You need this to operate an appliance. _____

Hidden Clue Puzzles 95

Name _____ Class _____ Date _____

Below are 15 clues for 15 words. Hint: Each word has alt *in it.*

1. To stop. _____
2. You put this in food. _____
3. This is made with milk and ice cream. _____
4. _____ Disney. _____
5. Another way or route. _____
6. A city in Maryland. _____
7. The height of a plane in the air. _____
8. To change something. _____
9. The part sung by the lowest female voice. _____
10. This is used in ale. _____
11. Any structure serving as a place of sacrifice or worship. _____
12. Completely; wholly; thoroughly. _____
13. A rope or strap used for leading or tying a horse or other animal.

   _____
14. To hesitate. _____
15. This is a person who is devoted to the interests of others.

   _____

Hidden Clue Puzzles 96

Below are ten clues for ten words. Hint: Each word has an animal in it.

1. Something that grows. _____
2. A king or queen wears this on his or her head. _____
3. To cut. _____
4. The growth of hair on the face of a man. _____
5. Part of your foot. _____
6. In a fraction, the term above the line. _____
7. In the metric system, a unit of weight. _____
8. Poisonous. _____
9. A short high-pitched tone used as a signal or warning.

   _____

10. The smallest particle of a substance that keeps the properties of the substance and is made up of one or more atoms. _____

Hidden Clue Puzzles 97

Below are ten clues for ten words. Hint: Each word has something to eat in it.

1. What something costs. _____
2. An insect with hard front wings. _____
3. Freedom from war or other disturbances. _____
4. A feather. _____
5. A loud, sharp, piercing cry. _____
6. To make a hole in or through. _____
7. Nourishment. _____
8. A weapon consisting of a long wooden shaft with a sharp point.

   _____
9. A person who seeks office. _____
10. To struggle against. _____

Hidden Clue Puzzles 98

Below are ten clues for ten words that have an animal in them. The word in parentheses tells you the kind of animal.

1. A fruit. (a wild animal) _____
2. A flower. (a desert animal) _____
3. Something you climb. (a snake) _____
4. Something that's cooked. (a night bird) _____
5. A listing of something in order. (a pet) _____
6. It holds things. (a domestic animal) _____
7. A slope. (an insect) _____
8. A city in Greece. (a domestic bird) _____
9. A faucet. (a domestic animal) _____
10. Doctrine. (a pet) _____

Hidden Clue Puzzles 99

Below are seven clues for seven words. Hint: Each word has pal *in it.*

1. Special dwelling. _____
2. Tree. _____
3. Part of the mouth. _____
4. Person of authority. _____
5. To beat rapidly. _____
6. Inferior. _____
7. To pierce. _____

Hidden Clue Puzzles 100

Below are eight clues for eight words. Hint: Each word contains cap.

1. Sleeveless garment. _____
2. Prank. _____
3. Ability. _____
4. Special building. _____
5. Confined. _____
6. Small blood vessel. _____
7. Surrender. _____
8. Changeable. _____

PART TWO

TEACHER'S GUIDE

section one

Guide to Selected Reading/Thinking Skills

Developing Selected Reading/Thinking Skills

Reading comprehension is a complex intellectual process involving a number of abilities. The two major abilities have to do with word meanings and reasoning with verbal concepts. Obviously, comprehension involves thinking. However, if teachers persist in asking only comprehension questions of a literal type, which demand a simple convergent answer that is explicitly stated in the book, higher-level thinking skills will not be developed. In this book students are presented with practices that require a higher level of thinking than that required by practices of a literal type.

The exercises in Section I concern reading/thinking skills that require reasoning with verbal concepts. A brief explanation of the selected reading/thinking skills presented in the section follows:

Skill 1. Finding the Main Idea or Central Idea:	Being able to supply the central thought of a paragraph, a group of paragraphs, an article, or a story by determining what the topic of the paragraph or group of paragraphs is and what is special about the topic. All sentences in the paragraph or all paragraphs in a story develop the main idea or the central idea. (*Main idea* is generally used when one talks about a paragraph, and *central idea* is generally used when one talks about a group of paragraphs, an article, or a story.)
Skill 2. Drawing Inferences or "Reading Between the Lines":	Being able to derive understanding from information that is not directly stated but is implied (indirectly stated).
Skill 3. Categorizing:	Being able to classify items into a more general group or to determine whether an item belongs in a specific group.
Skill 4. Completing Analogies:	Being able to discern relationships between words or ideas.
Skill 5. Following Directions:	Being able to read instructions and then carry them out.
Skill 6. Finding Inconsistencies:	Being able to supply the correct word by drawing a logical conclusion from the sentence or story material.
Skill 7. Distinguishing Between Fact and Opinion:	Being able to differentiate between information that can be verified and information that cannot be proved.
Skill 8. Detecting Propaganda Techniques and Bias:	Propaganda Techniques: Being able to determine the technique the writer is using to try to influence the reader to his or her view. Bias: Being able to detect a partiality or a slanting or something of that nature.
Skill 9. Using Divergent Thinking:	Being able to go beyond what the author has written to come up with new or alternate solutions.

Skill 1: Finding the Main Idea of a Paragraph or the Central Idea of a Story

Finding the Main Idea of a Paragraph

The main idea of a paragraph is the central thought of the paragraph. It's what the paragraph is about. Without a main idea, the paragraph would just be a confusion of sentences. All the sentences in the paragraph should develop the main idea.

To find the main idea of a paragraph, students must find what common element the sentences share. Some textbook writers place the main idea at the beginning of a paragraph and may actually put the topic of the paragraph in bold print in order to emphasize it. However, in literature this is not a common practice. In some paragraphs the main idea is not directly stated but implied; that is, the main idea is indirectly stated, and students have to find it from the clues given by the author.

Finding the Central Idea of a Story

The central idea of a story is the central thought of the story. All the paragraphs of the story should develop the central idea. To find the central idea of a story, students must find what common element the paragraphs in the story share. The introductory paragraph is usually helpful because it anticipates what the central idea is and how it will be developed. The procedure for finding the central idea of a story is similar to that of finding the main idea of a paragraph.

The presented exercises help students develop their ability to find the main idea of a paragaph and the central idea of a short story.

Objectives   ## Exercises

1. The students will be able to state the main idea of the paragraph.   1, 2, 3, 4, 5, 6

2. The student will be able to choose the statement that best expresses the main idea of the paragraph and explain why each of the other statements is not correct.   7

3. The student will be able to state the central idea of the given short story and supply a title for the short story that reflects the central idea of the story.   8, 9, 10

Exercise References

1. From Herbert S. Zim, "Sharks!" *Cricket* (July 1977), p. 68.
2. From George and Kay Schaller, "Lions on the Hunt," *Cricket* (August 1978), p. 35.
3. From Bob Trowbridge, "Fight Your Nightmares," *Cricket* (October 1978), p. 18.
4. From J.A. Hunter, African Hunter (New York: Harper & Brothers, 1952)

5. From *Tom Sawyer* by Mark Twain.
6. From *Why an Airplane Flies* by Wolfgang Langewiesche.
7. Adapted from Michael J. Mahoney and Kathryn Mahoney, "Fight Fat with Behavior Control," *Psychology Today* (May 1976).
8. From Leslie Forbes, "SOS in the Night," *Coronet* (June 1952).
9. Aesop's Fable, "You Can't Please Everybody."
10. "The Penny-Wise Monkey" in *More Jataka Tales;* retold by Ellen C. Babbitt (New York: Appleton-Century-Crofts, 1950).

Answers to the Exercises on Finding the Main Idea of a Paragraph or the Central Idea of a Story

EXERCISE 1 (p. 7)

Two different groups of sharks are described.

EXERCISE 2 (p. 8)

Lions hunt cooperatively.

EXERCISE 3 (p. 9)

The Senoi method may help you end your nightmares.

EXERCISE 4 (p. 10)

Leopards are now widely protected because they play an important part in maintaining nature's balance.

EXERCISE 5 (p. 11)

Aunt Polly was infatuated with patent medicines and all newfangled cures.

EXERCISE 6 (p. 12)

What makes an airplane fly is its shape.

EXERCISE 7 (p. 13)

The answer is statement 4. Statement 1 is a fact in the paragraph, but it is too specific to be the main idea. Statement 2 is too general. The paragraph is not discussing all persons. Statement 3 can be inferred from the paragraph, but it is not the main idea of the paragraph. Statement 5 is too general. Statement 4 is what the paragraph is about. The sentences in the paragraph elaborate this idea by giving examples of various recreations that are connected or associated with food.

EXERCISE 8 (p. 14)

A young boy, by using his head, is able to signal for help. Sample title: Using Your Head Can Save the Day

EXERCISE 9 (p. 16)

A man and his son learn that you cannot please everyone. Sample title: You Can't Please Everyone.

EXERCISE 10 (p.18)

Topics: a monkey; the king of a large rich country. Literal level central idea: A monkey lost all the peas he had because he tried to get one more, and the king of a large rich country didn't risk everything by trying to take over a small country. Symbolic level central idea that applies to both topics: It's foolish to risk a lot to gain a little or if you are greedy, you may lose everything. Sample title: Being Greedy Can Cost You Everything

Student Self-Evaluation Progress Report

Student's Name _____

Skill 1: Finding the Main Idea of a Paragraph or the Central Idea of a Story

Exercise Number	Date	Able to find main idea of a paragraph or central idea of a story	
		Yes	No
1			
2			
3			
4			
5			
6			
7			
8			
9			
10			

Skill 2: Drawing Inferences or "Reading Between the Lines"*

Many times writers do not directly state what they mean but present ideas in a more indirect, roundabout way. That is why inference is called the ability to read "between the lines." *Inference* is defined as *understanding that is not derived from a direct statement but from an indirect suggestion in what is stated.* Readers draw inferences from writings; authors make implications or imply meanings.

The ability to draw inferences is especially important in reading fiction, but it is necessary for nonfiction also. Authors rely on inference to make their stories more interesting and enjoyable. Mystery writers find inference essential to the maintenance of suspense in their stories. For example, Sherlock Holmes and Perry Mason mysteries are based on the ability of the characters to uncover evidence in the form of clues that are not obvious to others around them.

Inference is an important process that authors rely on. Good readers must be alert to the ways that authors encourage inference.

The presented exercises help students to develop their ability to draw inferences.

Objectives   Exercises

1. If enough evidence exists, students will be able to draw inferences about the given selections.   1

2. The students will be able to draw inferences about the given selections.   2, 3

3. The students will be able to draw inferences about the given statements.   4, 5

4. If enough evidence exists, the students will be able to determine whether statements are "true" or "false."   6, 7, 8, 9, 10

*Dorothy Rubin. *The Vital Arts—Reading and Writing* (New York: Macmillan, 1979).

Answers to the Exercises on Drawing Inferences

EXERCISE 1 (p. 22)

1. (e)—can't tell. It could be any season of the year. We do not know in which part of the country or world John is traveling. The trees could be leafless as a result of a forest fire, a disease, or some other cause.
2. (a) Approximately noon—if the sun is directly overhead, its approximately 12:00 noon.
   (b) Approximately 7:00 P.M.—The group started out at about 12:00 noon; the sun set about seven hours after the hikers had started out.
   (c) Twelve persons. One-third went back; eight were left; two-thirds equals eight; one-third equals four; $8 + 4 = 12$.
   (d) West. The sun sets in the west—the hikers were going toward the setting sun.
3. (e) Not enough information is given.

EXERCISE 2 (p. 24)

1. (a) No. There are no pine trees at the North or South Pole. (b) Officers. Guides would not talk about *their* men. Guides usually act as advisers. They do not make decisions. Trappers trap animals for fur. Also, it is stated that the fire had been made for them. Officers do not usually prepare the camp. (c) The term *retreat* would be a commander's term. Nothing was stated about a storm nor was anything stated or suggested about Indians. Hunters would not usually hunt under such adverse conditions. It is too cold to hunt big game, and hunters would very rarely lose so many lives.
2. White. The North Pole is the only place where a house can have southern exposure on all four sides. Bears at the North Pole are polar bears. Polar bears are white.

EXERCISE 3 (p. 26)

1. Dry, sunny day. Clue: dust; sun.
2. West. Clues: children walking toward mountain range; sun setting behind mountain range; sun sets in west.
3. Nine. Clues: six children remaining; one-third had turned back; two-thirds equals six; one-third must be three; $3 + 6 = 9$.
4. It was a contest. Clue: prize.
5. No. Clue: blisters on feet.

EXERCISE 4 (p. 28)

1. She probably needed more time on the test.
2. The "world of sawdust" is usually referred to as the circus.

3. She was probably an actress.
4. Jennifer is very popular and well-liked.

EXERCISE 5 (p. 29)

1. John and Mary don't like to do anything new or different.
2. Pat feels anxious and nervous.
3. The man seems to be trying to avoid recognition. He suspects that he is being followed.
4. Mrs. Beasley was probably a "strict" teacher, supervisor, or principal whom the children seemed to fear.
5. Mr. Brown is unabe to give clear orders. He is not a good office manager.
6. Mr. Davis may be the boss. Mr. Brown may question everyone about what he or she says. Mr. Davis may not be trusted because he spreads rumors.
7. Mrs. Seale is probably helpful, caring, patient, and sympathetic, whereas Mrs. Sloan is probably uncaring, unsympathetic, and not helpful. Mrs. Sloan may also be very critical and not very patient.

EXERCISE 6 (p. 31)

1. Can't tell.
2. True.
3. Can't tell.
4. True.
5. True.
6. Can't tell.
7. True.
8. Can't tell.
9. Can't tell (The little girl may have been stepping on the cracks out of spite.).

EXERCISE 7 (p. 32)

1. Can't tell.
2. Can't tell.
3. Can't tell.
4. True (if the sun is directly overhead, its about noon).
5. True (the person said that he or she craves human warmth).

EXERCISE 8 (p. 33)

1. Can't tell.
2. Can't tell.
3. False (some light is needed for a shadow).

4. True.
5. Can't tell.
6. True.
7. Can't tell.

EXERCISE 9 (p. 34)

1. Can't tell. Terry can be a name or a nickname for a male or a female.
2. True.
3. True.
4. Can't tell.
5. Can't tell.
6. True.
7. True. (The person tries to become "invisible" in each class.)
8. True.
9. False.
10. True.
11. False.
12. True

EXERCISE 10 (p. 36)

1. Can't tell.
2. Can't tell.
3. True.
4. Can't tell. (The person may be afraid of getting hurt.)
5. Can't tell.
6. Can't tell.
7. True.

Student Self-Evaluation Progress Report

Student's Name _____

Skill 2: Making Inferences or ''Reading Between the Lines''

Exercise Number	Date	Number Correct/Possible Number Correct*
1		(12)
2		(8)
3		(10)
4		(4)
5		(7)
6		(9)
7		(5)
8		(7)
9		(12)
10		(7)

*If an explanation is required for an answer, this is counted as another question.

Skill 3: Categorizing

The ability to divide items into categories is a very important thinking skill. As children advance through the grades, they should be developing the skill of categorizing, that is, children should be able to differentiate and group items into more complex categories. Primary-grade children should be able to categorize a cat as distinct from a mouse or a rabbit. They should be able to group cat, dog, and cow together as animals. As these children develop their thinking skills, they should be able to proceed from more generalized classifications to more specialized classifications.

The presented exercises should help students develop their ability to classify items into larger categories as well as their ability to make more specific classifications.

Objectives

Exercises

1. Students will be able to categorize the given words into a number of different categories. — 1, 2

2. Students will be able to choose a word or phrase from the word list that best describes a given group of words. — 3, 4

3. Students will be able to choose the word from each set that does not belong. — 5, 6, 7, 8, 9, 10, 11, 12

4. Students will be able to choose a word from the word list that belongs to each set. — 13

5. Students will be able to choose a word from the word list to complete each sentence and make the statement true. — 14, 15

Answers to the Exercises on Categorizing

EXERCISE 1 (p. 38)

Sample answers: **Animals**—dog, cat, chicken, horse, cow, tiger, gorilla, and so on. **Wild Animals**—tiger, gorilla, elephant, rhinoceros, hippopotamus. **Farm animals**—pig, chicken, cow, duck, turkey, cat, dog. **Jungle animals**—tiger, elephant, rhinoceros, hippopotamus, gorilla. **Pets**—dog, cat, horse. (Some children might have a duck as a pet.) **Domestic animals**—dog, cat. (Answers will vary.)

EXERCISE 2 (p. 39)

Sample Answers: **Books**—*Henry Huggins, Charlotte's Web, A History of the United States, The Study of the Earth, Cloth,* and so on. **Fiction Books**—*Charlotte's Web, Henry Huggins, Little Women.* **Non-fiction Books**—*Cloth, The Study of the Earth, Earthquakes, The Diary of a Young Girl, The Life of George Washington,* and so on. **Biographies**—*Young Man in the White House, The Life of George Washington.* **Autobiographies**—*The Diary of a Young Girl, The Story of My Life.* **Television Programs**—All in the Family, The Jeffersons, The Johnny Carson Show, Rockford Files, and so on. Other possible categories—**Adventure Books, Television Talk Shows, Television Adventure Shows, Books on Earth,** and so on. (Answers will vary.)

EXERCISE 3 (p. 40)

(1) books, (2) famous women, (3) animals, (4) transportation, (5) states, (6) Northeastern states, (7) parts of a fish, (8) parts of a horse, (9) parts of a bird, (10) dried fruit, (11) vegetables (12) male animals, (13) homes, (14) presidents, (15) nuts, (16) grains, (17) plants, (18) metal

EXERCISE 4 (p. 41)

(1) fruit, (2) food, (3) dairy products, (4) desserts, (5) meat, (6) female animals, (7) books, (8) nonfiction books, (9) fiction books, (10) wood products

EXERCISE 5 (p. 42)

(1)New Hampshire, (2) spider (not technically an insect), (3) trout, (4) porcupine, (5) shark (not an aquatic mammal), (6) nuts, (7) understand, (8) weary, (9) snail (not a snake), (10) matter

EXERCISE 6 (p. 43)

(1) Seattle, (2) heavy, (3) bell (not a characteristic cry or sound of a bird, insect or animal), (4) witch, (5) weary, (6) Siamese, (7) flies (do not have eight legs), (8) frogs (not reptiles), (9) San Francisco (not a capital), (10) stove

EXERCISE 7 (p. 44)

(1) pecan (not a cereal grain), (2) dam (not a male animal), (3) dame (not a young female), (4) hut (not an animal dwelling), (5) margarine (made primarily from vegetable oil), (6) rose (not grown from a bulbous herb), (7) capitalist (not a teacher), (8) station (not a special storage place), (9) drill (no blade), (10) rib (not an organ)

EXERCISE 8 (p. 45)

(1) serious, (2) lamb, (3) peas, (4) mare, (5) hen, (6) sire, (7) dust, (8) house, (9) snail (not a snake), (10) sturdy, (11) ambiguous, (12) indolent

EXERCISE 9 (p. 46)

(1) wings, (2) giraffe, (3) Angora, (4) closet, (5) astrology (a pseudoscience), (6) wolf (not of the cat family, (7) mare, (8) cowl, (9) sledge (a vehicle for carrying things over snow and ice), (10) raft

EXERCISE 10 (p. 47)

(1) drake, (2) India, (3) prune, (4) wasp, (5) cougars, (6) sextant, (7) anecdote, (8) beetles, (9) yacht, (10) trombone

EXERCISE 11 (p. 48)

(1) derby, (2) bunk (3) table, (4) Volkswagen, (5) dais, (6) New Jersey, (7) save, (8) ocean, (9) crocodile (a reptile), (10) sure

EXERCISE 12 (p. 49)

(1) symbol, (2) gregarious, (3) intense, (4) industrious, (5) delete, (6) spend-thrift, (7) decimate, (8) infinitesimal, (9) problem, (10) insecure, (11) obsessed, (12) sophomoric

EXERCISE 13 (p. 50)

(1) larva, (2) decade, (3) decimeter, (4) ticks (eight-legged), (5) butterflies (insects), (6) turtles (reptiles), (7) salamanders (amphibians), (8) asps (snakes), (9) squids (shellfish), (10) seal (aquatic mammal)

EXERCISE 14 (p. 51)

(1) day, (2) circle, (3) minute, (4) collies, (5) piglets, (6) triangle, (7) plants, (8) liquids, (9) kangaroos, (10) week, (11) chickens, (12) month, (13) apples, (14) insects, (15) lemons

EXERCISE 15 (p. 52)

(1) pound, (2) snakes, (3) onion, (4) animals, (5) ten, (6) humans, (7) herbivorous, (8) sun, (9) fluids, (10) moisture

Student Self-Evaluation Progress Report

Student's Name _____

Skill 3: Categorizing

Exercise Number	Date	Number Correct/Possible	Number Correct*
1			(6 or more)
2			(9 or more)
3			(18)
4			(10)
5			(10)
6			(10)
7			(10)
8			(12)
9			(10)
10			(10)
11			(10)
12			(12)
13			(10)
14			(15)
15			(10)

Skill 4: Completing Analogies

Analogies are word sets based on relationships. In order to supply the missing term in a proportion, people must know how the meanings of the words relate to each other. Example: prince is to princess as wizard is to _____ (witch).

Working with analogies requires high-level thinking skills. Students must have a good stock of vocabulary and the ability to see relationships. Students who have difficulty in classification will usually have difficulty working with analogies.

The presented exercises should help students in working with analogies.

Objective   Exercises

Students will be able to find the word from the word list to complete correctly each analogy.   1–15

Answers to the Exercises on Completing Analogies

EXERCISE 1 (p. 54)

(1) low, (2) hospital, (3) cold, (4) solid, (5) deer, (6) drake, (7) dollar, (8) grape, (9) spice, (10) bother, (11) assist, (12) self, (13) face

EXERCISE 2 (p. 55)

(1) short, (2) mare, (3) well, (4) scale, (5) clothing, (6) win, (7) singe, (8) cub, (9) warn, (10) least, (11) shout, (12) ten

EXERCISE 3 (p. 56)

(1)last, (2) sow, (3) wizard, (4) antonym, (5) quartet, (6) chase, (7) freeze, (8) transmission, (9) patient, (10) adept, (11) dry, (12) banking

EXERCISE 4 (p. 57)

(1) day, (2) chirp, (3) blizzard, (4) drove, (5) doe, (6) century, (7) ram, (8) love, (9) ecstasy, (10) binary, (11) kilometer, (12) meter, (13) pour, (14) ship, (15) compass

EXERCISE 5 (p. 58)

(1) raisin, (2) vegetable, (3) worst, (4) tepee, (5) mouth, (6) kid, (7) least, (8) Persian, (9) cyclone, (10) century, (11) strike, (12) bicentennial, (13) spike, (14) sudden, (15) charge

EXERCISE 6 (p. 59)

(1) solid, (2) frigid, (3) dollar, (4) seam, (5) prune, (6) adequate, (7) warn, (8) absorb, (9) transport, (10) powerful

EXERCISE 7 (p. 60)

(1) flower, (2) less, (3) hospital, (4) century, (5) plant, (6) belt, (7) disclose, (8) whack, (9) carry, (10) command

EXERCISE 8 (p. 61)

(1) quartet, (2) wizard, (3) epilogue, (4) lizard, (5) deny, (6) boulder, (7) scarf, (8) arrogant, (9) destroy, (10) pomposity

EXERCISE 9 (p. 62)

(1) tornado, (2) huge, (3) destroy, (4) grain, (5) instrument, (6) prepared, (7) posthaste, (8) organ, (9) attitude, (10) abyss

EXERCISE 10 (p. 63)

(1) adder, (2) pup, (3) veterinarian, (4) command, (5) stag, (6) mammoth, (7) ornithologist, (8) malign, (9) save, (10) million

EXERCISE 11 (p. 64)

(1) ecstatic, (2) hundred, (3) scorpions, (4) pistil, (5) taut, (6) trumpet, (7) compact, (8) insects, (9) shock, (10) naive

EXERCISE 12 (p. 65)

(1) fold, (2) stable, (3) falcon, (4) render, (5) quiver, (6) rake, (7) stub, (8) roe, (9) pay, (10) enough

EXERCISE 13 (p. 66)

(1) most, (2) obstinate, (3) artist, (4) moccasin, (5) signal, (6) arctic, (7) pacify, (8) dash, (9) antenna, (10) example

EXERCISE 14 (p. 67)

(1) aid, (2) deny, (3) latter, (4) century, (5) avocation, (6) epilogue, (7) arrest, (8) barren, (9) crypt, (10) vocation

EXERCISE 15 (p. 68)

(1) spectator, (2) spectacle, (3) pedestrian, (4) pediatrician, (5) biweekly, (6) automaton, (7) underwater, (8) unite, (9) duplicate, (10) friendly

Student Self-Evaluation Progress Report

Student's Name _____

Skill 4:   Completing Analogies

Exercise Number	Date	Number Correct/Possible Number Correct*
1		(13)
2		(12)
3		(12)
4		(15)
5		(15)
6		(10)
7		(10)
8		(10)
9		(10)
10		(10)
11		(10)
12		(10)
13		(10)
14		(10)
15		(10)

Skill 5: Following Directions

   Good direction followers do better on tests, answer questions better, and are better able to supply information. Here are some pointers for you, the teacher, that can help your students to be better in following directions.

1. Give your students practice in following directions.
2. Encourage students to ask questions about any direction that they are not sure of or that seems confusing to them.
3. Help your students to understand how important the skill of following directions is.
4. Help your students to understand that the ability to follow directions requires concentration.
5. Help students to *not* read into directions material that is not there.
6. Impress upon your students the importance of reading directions very carefully.

   The exercises that are presented in this book should help students become better direction followers. Note that some of the exercises ask students to read each set of directions *once* only because these exercises are stressing concentration.

Objectives   Exercises

1. The students will be able to read each numbered in-   1, 2, 5, 6,
   struction and carry it out on the boxed material.   7, 9, 10
2. The students will be able to read each numbered instruction and carry it out on the given circles.   3, 8
3. The students will be able to read each numbered instruction and carry it out on the Following Directions
   Sheet.   4

Answers to Exercises on Following Directions

EXERCISE 1 (p. 71)

⊡ ⊡ ○ ○ △ ◎ △ △ △ A C R̷ M 1 5 6 2 ○ ○

EXERCISE 2 (p. 72)

(1) Put a cross on *C.* (2) Circle 7, 4, 6. (3) Underline *over,* the opposite of *under, log,* which rhymes with *fog,* and *get, set,* which both rhyme. (4) Put a cross on 7, 4, 6, and circle 9, 8. (5) Do nothing. The number of double-digit numbers is equal to the number of single-digit ones. (6) Circle 75, 85, 55, 45, 5, and underline *U.*

EXERCISE 3 (p. 73)

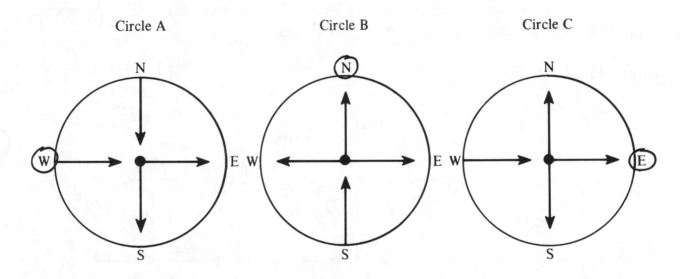

Circle A   Circle B   Circle C

EXERCISE 4 (p. 74)

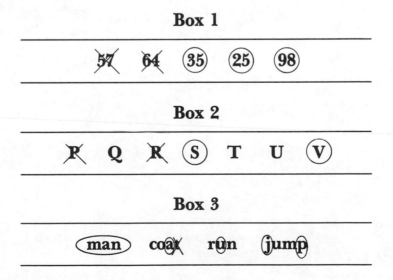

Box 1

5̷7̷ 6̷4̷ ㉟ ㉕ ㉘

Box 2

P̷ Q R̷ Ⓢ T U Ⓥ

Box 3

⟨man⟩ coa̷t̷ run ⟨jump⟩

299

EXERCISE 5 (p. 75)

(1) Put a line under *play*. (2) Put a circle around *big, stop,* and *man*. (3) Underline numbers 1 and 7. (4) Put a cross on the letters *M, N, O, P,* and *Q*. (5) Do nothing. There aren't three numbers that equal 16. (6) Put a circle around the numbers 63, 15, 1.

EXERCISE 6 (p. 76)

(1) Put a line over *short* and *coat*. (2) Put a line over *yellow*. (3) Put a line under 7. (4) Put a line over 5, 4, and 3. (5) Do nothing. There aren't four numbers one after the other that equal 20. (6) Circle the single-digit numbers 6 and 5 and the double-digit number 30. (7) Put a line under the Roman numeral X.

EXERCISE 7 (p. 77)

(1) Put a line under *run* and *fun*. (2) Put a check over *T*. (3) Underline 7 and 9. (4) Put a cross on *run,* a circle around *over,* and a line over *fill*. For numbers 5, 6, and 7, check answers by rereading directions.

EXERCISE 8 (p. 78)

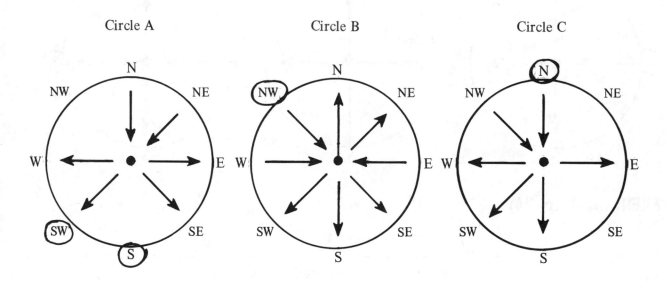

Circle A   Circle B   Circle C

EXERCISE 9 (p. 79)

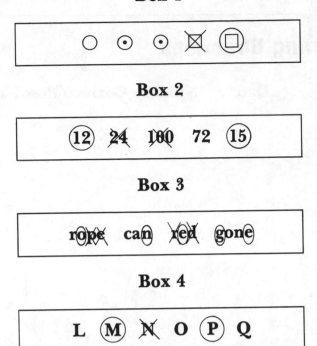

Box 1

Box 2

Box 3

Box 4

EXERCISE 10 (p. 80)

(1) Circle 6 and 4. (2) Circle the *v* in *give*. (3) Circle the *e* in *late*. (4) Circle *F*, the *t* in *let*, and *but*. (5) Put a cross on 10, 7, and 9 and *late*, *give*, and *but*.

Student Self-Evaluation Progress Report

Student's Name _____

Skill 5: Following Directions

Exercise Number	Date	Number Correct/Possible Number Correct*
1		(5)
2		(6)
3		(5)
4		(5)
5		(6)
6		(7)
7		(7)
8		(5)
9		(5)
10		(5)

*No credit is given if part of the answer is incorrect.

Skill 6: Finding Inconsistencies

Good thinkers are logical; that is, they are able to reason correctly. Finding inconsistencies refers to statements that do not make sense—they are illogical; they are not in accord with the given information.

The exercises on finding inconsistencies demand an alert reader. The reader is required to note any inconsistencies and then to supply the correct word by drawing a logical conclusion from the sentence or story material.

Objectives   ## Exercises

1. The students will be able to find the word in each sentence
   that does not make sense and replace it with one from the
   word list that does.   1, 2, 3
2. The students will be able to read the given paragraph and
   note any inconsistencies that exist in the paragraph.   4, 5

Answers to Exercises on Finding Inconsistencies

EXERCISE 1 (p. 82)

(1) setting—rising; (2) tame—wild; (3) dangerous—safe; (4) dawns—nights; (5) eggs—hay; (6) fools—foods; (7) Moses—Noah; (8) ship—plane; (9) feathers—fur; (10) gold—silver; (11) sweeten—season; (12) displeased—pleased

EXERCISE 2 (p. 83)

(1) chased, (2) picture, (3) role, (4) three, (5) insists, (6) elephant, (7) extinguishing, (8) spectacular, (9) thermometer, (10) interrupt

EXERCISE 3 (p. 84)

(1) interpreter, (2) intimidate, (3) interrogation, (4) intersession, (5) integral, (6) impatient, (7) covet, (8) indolent, (9) fawning, (10) obstinate

EXERCISE 4 (p. 85)

moon—sun; overcast—sunny; night—day; twice—once; two-thirds—two-fifths; southern—northern; famished—satiated; rising—setting; school—home; eastern—western; western—eastern

EXERCISE 5 (p. 86)

(1) An alien in the United States—he can't be both an American by birth and an alien. An alien is a foreigner. (2) Commander in the U.S. Air Force—a commander is an officer in the navy, not the air force. (3) An accomplished equestrian—means an accomplished horseman. (4) Disinterested scientists—they planned all year for the trip, so they can't be disinterested. (5) Banks of the Amazon—the tombs of the pharoahs are along the banks of the Nile. (6) Noted astrologists—the scientists were archaeologists. Astrologists are not scientists. (7) Watches—they didn't have watches thousands of years ago. (8) Unimpressed by the news—if the scientists had found something from thousands of years ago, they would be very excited. (9) North Pole—the banks of the Nile are toward the South Pole from the United States.

Student Self-Evaluation Progress Report

Student's Name _____

Skill 6: Finding Inconsistencies

Exercise Number	Date	Number Correct/Possible Number Correct*
1		(12)
2		(10)
3		(10)
4		(11)
5		(9)

Skill 7: Distinguishing Between Fact and Opinion

The ability to differentiate between facts and opinions is a very important skill that students need to develop. Often opinions are presented as though they are facts. Opinions are not facts. They are based on attitudes or feelings. Opinions can vary from individual to individual; they cannot be conclusively proved right or wrong. Facts, on the other hand, do not change from person to person to person. Facts are things that exist and can be proved true. Examples of facts: Albany is the capital of New York. Twelve inches equal a foot. A meter equals 39.37 inches. Examples of opinions: That is a pretty dress. He is very smart. It's important to visit museums.

Objective

The students will be able to determine whether a given statement is a fact or an opinion.

Exercises

1–5

Answers to Exercises on Distinguishing Between Fact and Opinion

EXERCISE 1 (p. 88)

(1) F, (2) O, (3) O, (4) O, (5) F, (6) O, (7) F, (8) O, (9) O, (10) F

EXERCISE 2 (p. 89)

(1) O, (2) O, (3) O, (4) F, (5) O, (6) F, (7) O, (8) O, (9) F, (10) O

EXERCISE 3 (p. 90)

(1) O, (2) O, (3) O, (4) F, (5) F, (6) O, (7) F, (8) O, (9) F, (10) O

EXERCISE 4 (p. 91)

(1) F, (2) O, (3) F, (4) O, (5) F, (6) F, (7) O, (8) F, (9) O, (10) O

EXERCISE 5 (p. 92)

(1) F, (2) F, (3) F, (4) F, (5) O, (6) F, (7) O, (8) F, (9) F, (10) O, (11) F, (12) O

Student Self-Evaluation Progress Report

Student's Name _____

Skill 7:   Distinguishing Between Fact and Opinion

Exercise Number	Date	Number Correct/Possible Number Correct*
1		(10)
2		(10)
3		(10)
4		(10)
5		(12)

Skill 8: Detecting Propaganda Techniques and Bias

Students should be helped to detect the presence of propaganda or bias in what they read.

Propaganda is defined as *any systematic, widespread, deliberate indoctrination* (the act of causing one to be impressed and eventually filled with some view) *or plan for indoctrination*. The term *propaganda* connotes deception or distortion. In other words, people who use propaganda are trying to influence persons by using deceptive methods.

Bias refers to a *mental leaning, a partiality, a prejudice,* or *a slanting of something*.

From the two definitions, you can see that persons interested in propagandizing something have a certain bias. They use propaganda techniques to distort information to indoctrinate people with their own views or bias.

1. Name calling: Accusing or denouncing an individual by using a widely disapproved label such as Red, Fascist, miser, reactionary, radical, and so on.
2. Glittering generalities: Seeking acceptance of ideas by resorting to terms generally accepted, such as freedom, American, Christian, red-blooded, democratic, businesslike, and so on.
3. Bandwagon: Seeking acceptance through appealing to pluralities. For example, an advertisement states: "*Most* persons perfer Dazzles. They know what's good! Do you?" In the "bandwagon" approach, you "go along" because everyone else is doing so.
4. Card stacking: Seeking acceptance by presenting or building on half-truths. Only favorable facts are presented, whereas anything unfavorable is deliberately omitted, and vice versa.
5. Transfer: Seeking acceptance by citing respected sources of authority, prestige, or reverence such as the home, the Constitution, the flag, the Church, and so on, in such a way as to make it appear that they approve the proposal. For example, in an advertisement, it is stated, "Our forefathers ate hearty breakfasts. Our country is built on strength. Our forefathers would want you to be strong. Eat Product X for strength. Product X will give you a hearty breakfast."
6. Plain folks: Seeking acceptance through establishing someone as "just one of the boys." Example: A presidential candidate is photographed milking cows, kissing babies, wearing work clothes, and so on.
7. Testimonial: Seeking acceptance by using testimonials from famous people to build confidence in a product. For example, in TV commercials, actors, athletes, and famous personalities are used to endorse a product.

The presented exercises are on detecting propaganda techniques and on determining the bias of writers.

Objectives   Exercises

1. The students will be able to identify the propaganda technique used in each of the sentences.   1, 2
2. The students will be able to identify the propaganda techniques used in a short selection.   3
3. The students will be able to determine whether the author is writing negatively or postively in each sentence.   4
4. The students will be able to determine whether the writer is neutral, has favorites, or is negative in each given headline.   5

309

Answers to Exercises on Detecting Propaganda Techniques and Bias

EXERCISE 1 (p. 94)

(1) testimonial, (2) bandwagon, (3) name calling, (4) glittering generalities, (5) testimonial, (6) name calling, (7) bandwagon, (8) glittering generalities, (9) testimonial, (10) glittering generalities

EXERCISE 2 (p. 95)

(1) bandwagon, (2) card stacking, (3) testimonial, (4) plain folks, (5) bandwagon, (6) name calling, (7) glittering generalities, (8) transfer, (9) card stacking, (10) name calling

EXERCISE 3 (p. 96)

(1) I was the only one not voting for his candidate—bandwagon;   (2) "True-Blue Tim"—glittering generalities;   (3) a student with lots of school spirit—glittering generalities;   (4) "Fathead Jane"—name calling;   (5) the majority of students are supporting—bandwagon;   (6) the famous local star thinks that Jane is the best person—testimonial;   (7) both their candidates are creeps—name calling; (8) because she is so democratic and fair—glittering generalities

EXERCISE 4 (p. 97)

(1) negative, (2) postive, (3) positive, (4) negative, (5) negative, (6) positive, (7) negative, (8) negative, (9) positive, (10) negative, (11) negative, (12) negative, (13) positive, (14) negative, (15) negative

EXERCISE 5 (p. 98)

1. (a) has a favorite (Jackson's team); (b) has a favorite (Jefferson's team); (c) neutral; (d) negative; (e) negative; (f) has a favorite (Jefferson's team)
2. (a) neutral; (b) has a favorite (Harrison); (c) has a favorite (Harrison); (d) neutral; (e) negative; (f) has a favorite (Harrison)

Student Self-Evaluation Progress Report

Student's Name _____

Skill 8: Detecting Propaganda Techniques and Bias

Exercise Number	Date	Number Correct/Possible Number Correct*
1		(10)
2		(10)
3		(8)
4		(15)
5		(12)

Skill 9: Using Divergent Thinking to Solve Problems

Divergent thinking has to do with the many different ways of looking at things. Good divergent thinkers are able to look beyond the obvious and come up with new or alternate solutions. Students should be encouraged to try to solve problems in many different ways and try to be intelligent risk-takers or make educated guesses.

The presented exercises should help students to become more divergent in their thinking.

Objective

The students will be able to solve the given problem by using divergent thinking.

Exercises

1–5

Student Self-Evaluation Progress Report

Student's Name _____

Skill 9: Using Divergent Thinking to Solve Problems

Exercise Number	Date	Number Correct/Possible Number Correct*
1		(7)
2		(5)
3		(5)
4		(4)
5		(3)

Answers to Exercises on Divergent Thinking

EXERCISE 1 (p. 100)

(1) One hour, unless you have a special clock that can be set for 24 h
alive. (3) Coins would not have been dated 46 B.C. because the birth
not anticipated at that time. (4) If he has a widow, he would be de
question of legality. (5) She's the woman's sister. (6) Nine. (7) 70; 3(
There are two halves to each whole; $30 \times 2 = 60$; $60 + 10 = 70$.

EXERCISE 2 (p. 101)

(1) Six. The answer is *not* in Roman numerals. (2) Yes. If you answer
were thinking of the holiday. (3) One. We have only one birthday,
many anniversaries to celebrate our birthday. (4) All have at least 28 d
(Take away the *s*, and it becomes even.)

EXERCISE 3 (p. 102)

(1) Two apples. (2) A 50-cent piece and a nickel—although "one" is no
"other" one is. (3) The match. (4) One hour. (5) There are 30 differe
each of 1×1; nine each of 2×2; four each of 3×3; and one ea

EXERCISE 4 (p. 103)

(1) The surgeon was a woman. (2) The football teams were composed
(3) The nurses and doctor were all males. (4) The supervisor was a f

EXERCISE 5 (p. 104)

1. The key is to go beyond the dots.

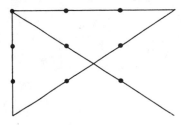

2. The victim was stabbed with an icicle.
3. The words that would fit would be in an alphabetical sequence, w
ceeding word having one extra letter, for example: A be car down
garages horrible.

section two

Guide to Vocabulary Expansion Skills

Developing Vocabulary Expansion Skills

Good vocabulary and good reading go hand in hand. Unless people know the meanings of words, they will have difficulty in understanding what they are reading. It should be stressed that just knowing the meaning of the word will not ensure that individuals will be able to state the meaning of the sentence, and knowing the meaning of the sentence does not also ensure that people can give the meaning of the paragraph, and so on. However, by not knowing the meaning of the word, individuals have considerably less chance of being able to read well. Without an understanding of words, comprehension is impossible.

As children advance in concept development, their vocabulary development must also advance because the two are interrelated. Children deficient in vocabulary will usually be deficient in concept development. Studies have shown that "vocabulary is a key variable in reading comprehension and is a major feature of most tests of academic aptitude . . ."*

Most teachers are aware of the importance of building sight vocabulary and word attack skills are a large part of the beginning reading program. However, the vocabulary development which concerns the building of a larger meaning vocabulary is often neglected.

As students become more advanced in reading, more words that previously only had one meaning are being met in new and strange situations. Starting at the intermediate grades, students should be guided to a mastery of vocabulary. If they are fascinated with words, they generally want to know the longest word in the dictionary, and many enjoy pronouncing funny or nonsense-sounding words such as "supercalifragilisticexpialidocious." These students should be helped to:

1. Become aware of words they do not know.
2. Try to guess the meaning from the context and their knowledge of combining forms (word parts).
3. Learn the most-used combining forms.
4. Jot down words that they do not know and look them up in the dictionary later.
5. Keep a notebook and write down the words they have missed in their vocabulary exercises, giving them additional study. Learn to break words down into combining forms (word parts) in order to learn their meaning.
6. Maintain interest in wanting to expand vocabulary.

The exercises in Section II concern the building of vocabulary. A brief explanation of the vocabulary expansion skills that are present in this section follows:

Skill 10. Using Combining Forms to Expand Vocabulary:	Being able to use combining forms to build a word and being able to figure out the meanings of words by knowing the meanings of combining forms.
Skill 11. Expanding Vocabulary with Homographs (Words with Multiple Meanings):	Being able to figure out the meanings of words that are spelled the same but have different meanings based on how they are used in the sentence.
Skill 12. Using Context Clues to Gain Word Meanings:	Being able to figure out the meaning of a word from the surrounding words in the sentence.
Skill 13. Expanding Vocabulary with Synonyms and Antonyms:	Being able to find words that are similar in meaning (synonyms) and being able to find words that are opposite in meaning (antonyms).

*Walter M. MacGinitie, "Language Development," *Encyclopedia of Educational Research*, 4th ed. (London: Collier-Macmillan, 1969), p. 693.

Skill 10: Using Combining Forms to Expand Vocabulary

Defining Combining Form Terms (Word Parts)

As a means of helping students to use combining forms as an aid to increasing vocabulary, some terms should be defined. There are a great number of words in our language that combine with other words to form new words, for example, *grandfather* and *policeman* (compound words). Many root (base) words are also combined with a letter or additional letters either at the beginning (prefix) or end (suffix) of the root (base) word, to form a new, related word; for example, *replay* and *played*. *Affix* is a term used to refer either to a prefix or a suffix.

In the words *replay* and *played, play* is a root or base, *re* is a prefix, and *ed* is a suffix. A *root* is the smallest unit of a word that can exist and retain its basic meaning. It cannot be subdivided any further. *Replay* is not a root word because it can be subdivided to *play. Play* is a root word because it cannot be divided further and still retain a meaning related to the "root" word.

Derivatives are combinations of root words with either prefixes or suffixes or both. *Combining forms* are usually defined as roots borrowed from another language that join together or that join with a prefix, a suffix, or both a prefix and a suffix to form a word. Many times the English combining form elements are derived from Greek and Latin roots. *In this book a combining form is defined as any word part that can join with another word or word part to form a word or a new word.*

Vocabulary Expansion Instruction

Vocabulary expansion instruction depends on the ability levels of students, their past experiences, and their interests. If they are curious about sea life and have an aquarium in the classroom, this could stimulate interest in such combining forms as *aqua*, meaning "water," and *mare* meaning "sea." The combining form *aqua* could generate such terms as *aquaplane, aqueduct,* and *aquanaut.* As *mare* means "sea," students could be given the combining forms *aquamarine* to define. Knowing the stems *aqua* and *marine*, many will probably respond with "sea water." The English term actually means bluish-green. The students can be challenged as to why the English definition of aquamarine is bluish-green.

A terrarium can stimulate discussion of words made up of the combining form *terra*.

When discussing the prefix *bi,* children should be encouraged to generate other words that also contain *bi,* such as *bicycle, binary, bilateral,* and so on. Other suggestions follow.

Write the words *biped* and *quadruped* in a column on the board, along with their meanings. These words should elicit guesses for groups of animals. The teacher could ask such questions as: "What do you think an animal that has eight arms or legs would be called?" "What about an animal with six feet?" And so on. When the animals are listed on the board, the children can be asked to look them up in the dictionary so that they can classify them.

For more discussion about combining forms, see Dorothy Rubin, *Gaining Word Power* (New York: Macmillan, 1978).

When presenting the combining forms *cardio, tele, graph,* and *gram,* place the following vocabulary words on the board:

cardiograph   telegraph
cardiogram   telegram

After students know that *cardio* means "heart" and *tele* means "from a distance," ask them to try to determine the meaning of *graph*, as used in *cardiograph* and *telegraph*. Have them try to figure out the meaning of *gram*, as used in *telegram* and *cardiogram*. Once students are able to define *graph* as an instrument or machine, and *gram* as message, they will hardly ever confuse a cardiograph with a cardiogram.

When students are exposed to such activities, they become more sensitive to their language. They come to realize that words are man-made, that language is living and changing, and that as people develop new concepts, they need new words to identify them. The words *astronaut* and *aquanaut* are good examples of words that came into being because of space and undersea exploration.

Objectives   ## Exercises

1. The students will be able to figure out the meaning of the combining form from words that are derived from the combining forms.   1

2. The students will be able to use the combining forms and their meanings to choose the word from the word list that best fits the blank in each sentence and define the word.   2, 3, 4, 5, 6, 7

3. The students will be able to use the combining forms and their meanings to figure out the meanings of the underlined words and to build a word that will fit the blank in each sentence.   8

4. The students will be able to use the combining forms and their meanings to figure out the meanings of the words in the word list and then to choose the word that best fits the blank in each sentence.   9, 10

Answers to Exercises on Combining Forms

EXERCISE 1 (p. 109)

A. (1) two, (2) year, (3) life, (4) study or science of, (5) hundred, hundredth part of, (6) self, (7) something written, (8) foot, (9) say, (10) see

B. (1) f, (2) j, (3) e, (4) a, (5) b, (6) c, (7) g, (8) i, (9) d, (10) h

EXERCISE 2 (p. 110)

(1) bicycle—two-wheeler; (2) biology—study of life; (3) chronological—referring to time; (4) biped—two-footed animal; (5) pediatrician—children's doctor; (6) century—period of 100 years; (7) podiatrist—foot doctor; (8) decade—period of ten years; (9) cyclone—strong, destructive whirlwinds

EXERCISE 3 (p. 111)

(1) Bigamy (marriage to two persons at the same time); legal (lawful); (2) Monogamy (marriage to one at one time); (3) monarchy (a form of government in which there is rule by a single person, such as a king, queeen, or emperor); monarch (a ruler in a monarchy such as a king, queen, or emperor); (4) Theocracy (a form of government in which there is rule by a religious group); (5) legislature (a body of persons responsible for making laws for a state or country); (6) autocracy (a form of government in which the ruler has absolute control); autocrat (an absolute ruler); (7) atheist (one who does not believe in the existence of God); (8) anarchy (without rule).

EXERCISE 4 (p. 112)

Meanings: finish = to end; infinite = not ending; credible = believable; incredible = not believable; microscope = an instrument to see very small objects; telescope = an instrument used to see things from afar; auditorium = place for listening; inaudible = not able to be heard; audience = persons listening

(1) audience, (2) microscope, (3) telescope, (4) infinite, (5) finish, (6) incredible, (7) (a)inaudible, (b) auditorium, (8) credible

EXERCISE 5 (p. 113)

(1) invisible—not able to be seen; (2) visible—able to be seen; (3) alias—another name; (4) alien—foreigner; (5) alienate—make others unfriendly; (6) inalienable —not able to be taken away; (7) potent—powerful; (8) impotent—powerless; (9) potentate—ruler, very powerful person; (10) potential—possible ability

EXERCISE 6 (p. 114)

(1) omnipotent—all-powerful; omniscient—all-knowing; (2) potent—powerful; (3) science—any area of knowledge in which the facts have been investigated and presented in an orderly manner; (4) logical—relating to the science concerned with correct reasoning; (5) convention—a formal meeting of members for political or professional purposes; (6) prologue—an introduction; (7) convenient—well-suited to one's purpose; (8) convene—come together or assemble; (9) omnipresent—being present everywhere at all times

EXERCISE 7 (p. 116)

(1) mobile—movable; (2) motive—what prompts someone to do something or act in a certain way; (3) motor—engine; (4) demoted—put in a lower rank; (5) promoted—advanced to the next higher grade; (6) motion—movement; (7) immobile—motionless; (8) automobile—a passenger vehicle; (9) automotive—self-propelling; (10) mobilized—assembled into readiness for action

EXERCISE 8 (p. 117)

Part A. (1) walkers, (2) one hundredth, (3) period of 100 years, (4) one thousand thousands—1,000,000, (5) study of earth's makeup, (6) poisonous, (7) study of the stars, (8) reading of the stars; false science, (9) without feet, (10) foot doctor

Part B. (1) autograph—signature; (2) aquanaut—one who explores undersea; (3) decade—period of ten years; (4) aquarium—a tank or glass globe that holds water plants and animals; (5) astronaut—one who explores outer space; (6) biology—study of living things; (7) telescope—instrument to view things from a distance; (8) bicentennial—two-hundredth anniversary; (9) autobiography—life story written by oneself; (10) geography—study of the earth's surface involving countries, continents, and so on

EXERCISE 9 (p. 119)

(1) gratified, (2) prejudiced, (3) congratulated, (4) judicious, (5) gratuity, (6) gratuitous, (7) gratitude, (8) ingrate

EXERCISE 10 (p. 120)

(1) impulsive, (2) expel, (3) propel, (4) repellent, (5) dispel, (6) compel, (7) repelled, (8) pulse

Student Self-Evaluation Progress Report

Student's Name _____

Skill 10:   Using Combined Forms to Expand Vocabulary

Exercise Number	Date	Number Correct/Possible Number Correct*
1		(20)
2		(9)
3		(11)
4		(9)
5		(10)
6		(10)
7		(10)
8		(20)
9		(8)
10		(8)

*Only half credit is given if a definition is required, and it is not correct, even though the correct word has been chosen.

Skill 11: Expanding Vocabulary with Homographs

Words that are spelled the same but have different meanings are called *homographs*. Because many words have more than one meaning, teachers need to help students to recognize that the meaning of the word is determined by its use in a sentence.

The presented activities challenge students to recognize that some words are spelled the same but have different meanings determined by their placement in a sentence.

Special Note

Confusion may exist among the terms *homonym, homophone,* and *homograph* because some authors are using the more scientific or linguistic definition for the terms and others are using the more traditional definition. *Homonyms* have traditionally been defined as words that sound alike, are spelled differently, and have different meanings; for example, *red, read.* However, many linguists use the term *homophone* rather than homonym for this meaning. Linguists generally use the term *homonym* for words, which are spelled the same, pronounced the same, but have different meanings; for example, *bat* (the mouselike winged mammal) and *bat* (the name for a club used to hit a ball.) *Bat* (baseball bat) and *bat* (animal) would traditionally be considered a homograph (words that are spelled the same but have different meanings), but linguists usually define *homographs* as words that are spelled the same but have *different pronunciations* and *different meanings;* for example, *lead* (dense metal) and *lead* (verb).

The teacher should be aware that different textbooks in language arts may be defining the three terms somewhat differently and should be familiar with the various systems and definitions in use. An attempt to find out which terms students have been exposed to and continued use of them will establish consistency, at least until pupils are old enough to understand the differences.

In this book the generic definition of homograph is used; that is, homographs are words which are spelled the same but have different meanings and the words may or may not be pronounced the same.

Objectives   Exercises

1. The students will be able to find one word for each
   sentence that fits in all its blanks.   1–11
2. The students will be able to find one word for each set of
   phrases that fits in all its blanks.   12, 13, 14, 15, 16
3. The students will be able to find one word that fits each
   set of multiple meanings.   17, 18, 19
4. The students will be able to find the one word that fits in
   each set of sentences and then give the meaning of the
   word as it is used in each different sentence.   20

Answers to Exercises on Homographs

EXERCISE 1 (p. 123)

(1) can, (2) loaf, (3), chest, (4) groom, (5) stamp, (6) mine, (7) slide, (8) sound, (9) tire, (10) fire

EXERCISE 2 (p. 124)

(1) fall, (2) fair, (3) jack, (4) plain, (5) past, (6) study, (7) belt, (8) meet, (9) fly, (10) stump.

EXERCISE 3 (p. 125)

(1) grade, (2) run, (3) mind, (4) coach, (5) plain, (6) hit, (7) duty, (8) band, (9) change, (10) watch

EXERCISE 4 (p. 126)

(1) park, (2) chap, (3) center, (4) mark, (5) major, (6) boxer, (7) float, (8) tip, (9) title, (10) seal

EXERCISE 5 (p. 127)

(1) blank, (2) pounds, (3) case, (4) breed, (5) spirits, (6) plot, (7) grill, (8) stand, (9) bone, (10) form

EXERCISE 6 (p. 128)

(1) show, (2) fast, (3) guard, (4) column, (5) present, (6) sports, (7) spot, (8) palm, (9) cross, (10) habit

EXERCISE 7 (p. 129)

(1) fair, (2) high, (3) set, (4) pick, (5) blow, (6) fool, (7) duck, (8) frank, (9) tire, (10) prunes

EXERCISE 8 (p. 130)

(1) note, (2) novel, (3) fit, (4) fine, (5) bear, (6) pupils, (7) shed, (8) pale (also means "picket" or "stake"), (9) rash, (10) down

EXERCISE 9 (p. 131)

(1) content, (2) capital, (3) train, (4) rest, (5) point, (6) chief, (7) compose, (8) breed, (9) present, (10) grain

EXERCISE 10 (p. 132)

(1) hose, (2) drain, (3) rose, (4) sign, (5) ball, (6) hail, (7) blind, (8) trial, (9) base, (10) crank

EXERCISE 11 (p. 133)

(1) part, (2) pass, (3) nice, (4) mold, (5) bridge, (6) grounded, (7) object, (8) bluff, (9) project, (10) position

EXERCISE 12 (p. 135)

(1) roll, (2) stem, (3) score, (4) fast, (5) slight, (6) snap, (7) rash, (8) steer, (9) last, (10) wrench

EXERCISE 13 (p. 136)

(1) belt, (2) boot, (3) border, (4) lime, (5) rattle, (6) stable, (7) stack, (8) tone, (9) tie, (10) trade

EXERCISE 14 (p. 137)

(1) root, (2) snap, (3) pepper, (4) foot, (5) grind, (6) operation, (7) bail, (8) balance, (9) concrete, (10) rule

EXERCISE 15 (p. 138)

(1) pin, (2) bond, (3) flat, (4) mean, (5) pit, (6) pitcher, (7) game, (8) race, (9) turn *or* tack, (10) point

EXERCISE 16 (p. 139)

(1) can, (2) train, (3) common, (4) fork, (5) stick, (6) draw, (7) pine, (8) ring, (9) interest, (10) plate, (11) pack, (12) pool, (13) plant, (14) post, (15) drove

EXERCISE 17 (p. 140)

(1) cast, (2) bark, (3) fly, (4) brush, (5) pole, (6) head, (7) position, (8) mean, (9) pitch, (10) crank

EXERCISE 18 (p. 141)

(1) pen, (2) fan, (3) dam, (4) dart, (5) steer, (6) clutch, (7) beam, (8) brood, (9) felt, (10) peer

EXERCISE 19 (p. 142)

(1) glasses, (2) pants, (3) pick, (4) board, (5) tape, (6) bloom, (7) reference, (8) crane, (9) signs, (10) plant, (11) court, (12) slip, (13) course, (14) slight, (15) deck

EXERCISE 20 (p 144)

Set I—run; (1) rip, (2) campaign as a candidate for election, (3) move with haste, (4) close competition

Set II—point; (1) a specific moment, (2) idea or what you want to get across, (3) a piece of land projecting into a body of water, (4) sharp end

Set III—scale; (1) a succession of steps, (2) a succession of tones going up or down according to fixed intervals, (3) a hard, bony plate covering, (4) a balance for weighing

Student Self-Evaluation Progress Report

Student's Name _____

Skill 11: Expanding Vocabulary with Homographs

Exercise Number	Date	Number Correct/Possible Number Correct*
1		(10)
2		(10)
3		(10)
4		(10)
5		(10)
6		(10)
7		(10)
8		(10)
9		(10)
10		(10)
11		(10)
12		(10)
13		(10)
14		(10)
15		(10)
16		(15)
17		(10)
18		(10)
19		(15)
20		(12)

Skill 12: Using Context Clues to Gain Word Meanings

Context clues help students to gain the meanings of unfamiliar words. By *context* we mean the words surrounding a word that can throw light on its meaning.

Teachers need to help students to be aware of the various clues that writers give to help readers gain the meaning of less familiar words. Some textbook writers will define, describe, or explain a word to make sure that readers get the meaning. Some other techniques that writers use are comparison and contrast and examples. (See the following section on synonyms and antonyms.)

The presented exercises should help students to develop their ability to use context clues.

Objectives   ## Exercises

1. The students will be able to choose one word from the word list to complete each sentence so that the sentence makes sense.   1, 10

2. The students will be able to use context clues to determine the feelings of the person in each sentence and then choose a word from the word list that best expresses the feeling.   2

3. The students will be able to use context clues to determine the meaning of the underlined word in each sentence.   3

4. The students will be able to use context clues to supply a word that makes sense in the sentence in place of the nonsense word.   4

5. The students will be able to use context clues to unscramble all the underlined words so that the story makes sense.   5, 6, 7

6. The students will be able to fill in each blank with a word so that the story makes sense   8, 9

Answers to Exercises on Context Clues

EXERCISE 1 (p. 147)

(1) run, (2) flowed, (3) box, (4) browse, (5) iron, (6) pine, (7) pinch, (8) spectacles, (9) posture, (10) idle, (11) suit, (12) blade, (13) rose, (14) bore, (15) fast

EXERCISE 2 (p. 148)

(1) embarrassed, (2) sad *or* disappointed, (3) disappointed *or* sad, (4) ashamed, (5) ecstatic, (6) frustrated, (7) insulted, (8) peculiar, (9) guilty, (10) anxious

EXERCISE 3 (p. 149)

(1) comes before, (2) receiver, (3) double, (4) careful, thorough, (5) brothers or sisters, (6) resistance to fatigue, (7) steal in small quantities, (8) frank, (9) wordy, (10) dressed

EXERCISE 4 (p. 150)

Sample answers: (1) monkey, (2) pier, (3) dog, (4) eat, (5) sport, (6) disappointed, (7) rescued, (8) telephone, (9) listen, (10) haunted

EXERCISE 5 (p. 151)

(1) they, (2) living, (3) ten, (4) moved, (5) forest, (6) city, (7) too, (8) for, (9) kind, (10) old, (11) made, (12) their, (13) selling, (14) baked, (15) breads, (16) cakes, (17) who, (18) to, (19) visit, (20) forest, (21) couple, (22) also, (23) help, (24) anyone, (25) needed, (26) it, (27) came, (28) the, (29) always, (30) the

EXERCISE 6 (p. 152)

(1) later, (2) beneath, (3) pine, (4) had, (5) nest, (6) tree, (7) there, (8) eggs, (9) duck, (10) her, (11) day, (12) came, (13) nest, (14) mother, (15) flap (16) and, (17) quacking, (18) three, (19) we, (20) awakened, (21) noise, (22) outside, (23) greeted, (24) five, (25) ducklings, (26) proud, (27) duck, (28) leading, (29) to, (30) stream

EXERCISE 7 (p. 153)

(1) cat, (2) cat, (3) eat, (4) rats, (5) plays, (6) eats, (7) food, (8) eat, (9) rat, (10) came, (11) live, (12) house, (13) Our, (14) cat, (15) its, (16) trap, (17) rat, (18) our, (19) cat, (20) peek, (21) trap, (22) saw, (23) grab, (24) bite, (25) trap, (26) rat, (27) also, (28) reward, (29) took, (30) bite, (31) trap, (32) both, (33) took, (34) nap, (35) on, (36) top, (37) counter, (38) never, (39) catch, (40) rat, (41) our, (42) trap

EXERCISE 8 (p. 154)

(1) moon, (2) deal, (3) from, (4) life, (5) you, (6) of, (7) on, (8) year, (9) days *or* mornings, (10) at, (11) She, (12) her, (13) and, (14) the, (15) on, (16) moon, (17) a, (18) the, (19) a, (20) takes, (21) clothing, (22) her, (23) and, (24) room, (25) her, (26) to, (27) what, (28) things, (29) will, (30) and

EXERCISE 9 (p. 155)

(1) game, (2) between, (3) High, (4) Yorktown, (5) game, (6) important, (7) each, (8) an, (9) The, (10) tie, (11) for, (12) was, (13) gym, (14) last, (15) in, (16) The, (17) crowded, (18) seats, (19) entered, (20) there, (21) cheers, (22) spectators, audience, *or* crowd, (23) its, (24) shooting, (25) sounded *or* rang, (26) in, (27) threw, (28) air, (29) in, (30) out, (31) was, (32) voice, (33) announced, (34) to, (35) power, (36) place, (37) told, (38) were

EXERCISE 10 (p. 156)

(1) capital, (2) ecstasy, (3) brief, (4) inquisitive, (5) lethal, (6) frustrated, (7) covert, (8) tactful, (9) fatigue, (10) crafty

Student Self-Evaluation Progress Report

Student's Name _____

Skill 12:   Using Context Clues to Gain Word Meanings

Exercise Number	Date	Number Correct/Possible Number Correct *
1		(15)
2		(10)
3		(10)
4		(10)
5		(30)
6		(30)
7		(42)
8		(30)
9		(38)
10		(10)

Skill 13: Expanding Vocabulary with Synonyms and Antonyms

Synonyms are different words that have almost the same meaning. Often words may be defined by other words of similar and more familiar meaning. For example, *indolent* is defined as *lazy*, and *dire* is defined as *extreme*.

Antonyms are words opposite in meaning to others. Examples: *obese—emaciated; delicate—coarse.*

Teachers should help their students to recognize that writers use synonyms and antonyms to make their writing clearer, more expressive, more informative, and more interesting.

The presented exercises should help students develop skill in working with synonyms and antonyms.

Objectives   Exercises

1. The students will be able to find another word from the word list that has the same meaning as the underlined word in the sentence.   1, 2, 3, 4

2. The students will be able to find a word from the word list that is similar in meaning to the given words.   5

3. The students will be able to choose a word from each set that is most similar to the first word.   6, 7

4. The students will be able to find a word from the word list that has the opposite meaning of the underlined word in each sentence.   8, 9

5. The students will be able to choose a word from each set that is opposite in meaning to the word at the beginning of the set.   10

Answers to Exercises on Synonyms and Antonyms

EXERCISE 1 (p. 158)

(1) large, (2) plump, (3) well-known, (4) drowsy, (5) snug, (6) head, (7) journey, (8) location, (9) passage, (10) perilous

EXERCISE 2 (p. 159)

(1) scent, (2) content, (3) wizard, (4) notorious, (5) posture, (6) raze, (7) grave, (8) jeopardy, (9) flinch, (10) significant

EXERCISE 3 (p. 160)

(1) huge, (2) exhausted, (3) equivalent, (4) annual, (5) capital, (6) sufficient, (7) group, (8) immature, (9) intimidate, (10) remedy

EXERCISE 4 (p. 161)

(1) beautiful, (2) skinny, (3) famished, (4) exhausted, (5) brilliant, (6) obese, (7) potent, (8) affluent, (9) ecstatic, (10) diligent, (11) terse, (12) discreet, (13) frigid, (14) spectacular, (15) immense

EXERCISE 5 (p. 162)

(1) torrid, (2) exhausted, (3) brilliant, (4) huge, (5) obese, (6) ancient, (7) satiated, (8) saturated, (9) parched, (10) emaciated, (11) posthaste, (12) dogged

EXERCISE 6 (p. 163)

(1) starved, (2) satisfied, (3) haughty, (4) economical, (5) wise, (6) change, (7) extreme, (8) concise, (9) desire, (10) shorten, (11) delay, (12) leaning

EXERCISE 7 (p. 164)

(1) punish, (2) destiny, (3) stick, (4) forgetful, (5) erase, (6) emigration, (7) doubtful, (8) believable, (9) faker, (10) miserable, (11) desiring, (12) warn

EXERCISE 8 (p. 165)

(1) shortest, (2) most, (3) worst, (4) less, (5) cleanest, (6) fastest, (7) tame, (8) complex, (9) modern, (10) naive

EXERCISE 9 (p. 166)

(1) confusing, (2) prudent, (3) humble, (4) different, (5) brief, (6) punctual, (7) densely, (8) polite, (9) curtail, (10) fickle

EXERCISE 10 (p. 167)

(1) more, (2) unimportant, (3) begin, (4) open, (5) powerful, (6) pessimist, (7) excessive, (8) evasive, (9) naive, (10) verbose, (11) understated, (12) stable

Student Self-Evaluation Progress Report

Student's Name _____

Skill 13: Expanding Vocabulary with Synonyms and Antonyms

Exercise Number	Date	Number Correct/Possible Number Correct*
1		(10)
2		(10)
3		(10)
4		(15)
5		(12)
6		(12)
7		(12)
8		(10)
9		(10)
10		(12)

section three

Guide to Fun with Words: Word Riddles and Word Puzzles

"Fun with Words" is a special section that your students should find challenging and enjoyable. Similar activities are grouped together and based on graduated levels of difficulty within each group. However, you should feel free to change the order to any sequence that you feel will better suit the needs of your students.

The objectives for each similar group of activities state the various skills included in the groups of activities.

Objectives   Exercises

1. The students will be able to use reasoning ability and vocabulary skills in following directions to solve the different word riddles.1-20

    1-20

2. The students will be able to use vocabulary skills, spelling skills, and following-direction skills to solve the various word puzzles.

    21-44

3. The students will be able to use visual discrimination, vocabulary skills, and spelling skills to find the required number of words or the special words in each word square or word rectangle puzzle.

    45-55

4. The students will be able to use visual discrimination, following-directions skills, and synthesis skills to solve each of the word riddle puzzles.

    56-65

5. The students will be able to use auditory and/or visual discrimination and vocabulalry skills to solve the rhyming word puzzles.

    66-72

6. The students will be able to use visual discrimination, vocabulary skills, spelling skills, and synthesis skills to solve each scrambled word puzzle.

    73-84

7. The students will be able to use visual discrimination, spelling skills, vocabulary skills, and categorizing skills to solve the hidden word puzzles.

    85-90

8. The students will be able to use visual discrimination skills, vocabulary skills, spelling skills, and categorizing skills to solve the hidden clue puzzles.

    91-100

Answers to Fun with Words: Word Riddles and Word Puzzles

WORD RIDDLES 1 (p. 171)

(1) drape—ape; (2) draw—drawl;; (3) nick—nickel; (4) flock—lock

WORD RIDDLES 2 (p. 172)

(1) mustard—must; (2) close—closet; (3) heart—hurt; (4) carpet—car; (5) sing—singe

WORD RIDDLES 3 (p. 173)

(1) bell—boy—bellboy; (2) blue—bird—bluebird; (3) pocket—book—pocketbook; (4) ice—land—Iceland; (5) rain—bow—rainbow

WORD RIDDLES 4 (p. 174)

(1) rear—ear; (2) air—hair; (3) bread—read; (4) ice—police; (5) bridle—bride; (6) closet—close; (7) pig—big

WORD RIDDLES 5 (p. 175)

(1) ice—rice; (2) cupid—cup; (3) butt—button; (4) brother—broth; (5) ant—plant; (6) denim—den; (7) boat—boa; (8) scent—cent; (9) bunny—bun; (10) pen—penny

WORD RIDDLES 6 (p. 176)

(1) joke—yolk; (2) globe—lobe; (3) peacock—pea; (4) monkey—key; (5) mold—old

WORD RIDDLES 7 (p. 177)

(1) ballon—ball; (2) beard—ear; (3) brains—rain; (4) pillow—pill; (5) moth—mother

WORD RIDDLES 8 (p. 178)

(·1) pear—ear; (2) oats—boats; (3) ouch—couch; (4) cabin—cab; (5) branch—ranch

WORD RIDDLES 9 (p. 179)

(1) arm—farm; (2) blink—link; (3) inch—cinch; (4) park—ark—lark; (5) limb—climb; (6) beagle—eagle

WORD RIDDLES 10 (p. 180)

(1) clown—frown; (2) clove—love; (3) lad—glad; (4) rush—thrush

WORD RIDDLES 11 (p. 181)

(1) loom—bloom; (2) twine—twin; (3) evil—devil; (4) pitch—itch

WORD RIDDLES 12 (p. 182)

(1) drug—rug; (2) oak—land—Oakland; (3) drag—on—dragon; (4) tease—ease; (5) rode—erode

WORD RIDDLES 13 (p. 183)

(1) den—mark—Denmark; (2) car—rot—carrot; (3) ma—lice—malice; (4) gram—mar—grammar

WORD RIDDLES 14 (p. 184)

(1) new—ark—Newark; (2) err—and—errand; (3) kid—nap—kidnap; (4) cap—rice—caprice

WORD RIDDLES 15 (p. 185)

(1) wing—swing; (2) block—lock; (3) latter—platter; (4) scat—cat; (5) lank—blank

WORD RIDDLES 16 (p. 186)

(1) plate—late; (2) towel—tow; (3) clam—clamp; (4) praise—raise; (5) den—maiden; (6) Magi—magic

WORD RIDDLES 17 (p. 187)

(1) climb—limb; (2) fox—ox; (3) imp—limp; (4) lass—class

WORD RIDDLES 18 (p. 188)

(1) doe—dove; (2) bear—beard; (3) fan—fang; (4) ale—kale; (5) reed—greed

WORD RIDDLES 19 (p. 189)

(1) slip, (2) bulb, (3) grill, (4) clog

WORD RIDDLES 20 (p. 190)

(1) tank, (2) rib, (3) cape, (4) key

WORD PUZZLES 21 (p. 191)

(1) pup, (2) dad *or* pop, (3) tot, (4) eye, (5) gag, (6) ewe, (7) bib, (8) nun

WORD PUZZLES 22 (p. 192)

(1) paper, (2) eraser, (3) error, (4) original, (5) alone, (6) nest, (7) star, (8) arithmetic, (9) ice, (10) cent

WORD PUZZLES 23 (p. 193)

(1) period, (2) odor, (3) orange, (4) gentle, (5) lemon, (6) one, (7) never, (8) error, (9) oriole, (10) letter, (11) era, (12) raison, (13) once, (14) cease, (15) seam

WORD PUZZLES 24 (p. 194)

(1) banana, (2) name, (3) meat, (4) athlete, (5) tease, (6) seam, (7) amuse, (8) semester, (9) erratic, (10) ice, (11) century, (12) rye, (13) yesterday, (14) aye, (15) yellow, (16 owl

WORD PUZZLES 25 (p. 195)

(1) please, (2) lease, (3) least, (4) east, (5) beast, (6) feast, (7) fast, (8) last, (9) lass, (10) glass, (11) class

WORD PUZZLES 26 (p. 196)

(1) sire, (2) eel, (3) lion, (4) nightmare, (5) elm, (6) map, (7) palm, (8) mansion, (9) nectarine, (10) elephant

WORD PUZZLES 27 (p. 197)

(1) tall, (2) bird, (3) thin, (4) glad, (5) down, (6) slip, (7) cake, (8) bike, (9) deer, (10) rice, (11) bean, (12) pear, (13) worm, (14) pine, (15) root

WORD PUZZLES 28 (p. 198)

(1) fall, (2) ball, (3) bald, (4) bale, (5) tale, (6) male, (7) mall, (8) mill, (9) mile, (10) mole, (11) mold, (12) gold, (13) golf, (14) wolf

WORD PUZZLES 29 (p. 199)

(1) frame, (2) flame, (3) blame, (4) blaze, (5) glaze, (6) graze, (7) grade, (8) trade, (9) trace, (10) track, (11) crack

WORD PUZZLES 30 (p. 200)

(1) garden, (2) enter, (3) erase, (4) season, (5) one, (6) necessary, (7) rye,

(8) yellow, (9) owe, (10) wealth, (11) thermometer, (12) eruption, (13) Ontario, (14) Iowa, (15) Washington

WORD PUZZLES 31 (p. 201)

(1) train, (2) brain, (3) braid, (4) brand, (5) bland, (6) blond, (7) blood, (8) bloom, (9) broom, (10) groom

WORD PUZZLES 32 (p. 202)

(1) noon, (2) reader, (3) toot, (4) peep, (5) deed, (6) madam, (7) level, (8) radar, (9) series, (10) retriever, (11) tenet

WORD PUZZLES 33 (p. 203)

(1) headache, (2) George, (3) shush, (4) church, (5) eraser, (6) onion, (7) decade, (8) photograph, (9) terminate, (10) temperate, (11) papa, (12) educated

WORD PUZZLES 34 (p. 204)

(1) onion, (2) mama, (3) escapes, (4) phonograph, (5) shellfish, (6) teammate, (7) eraser, (8) periscope, (9) emblem, (10) estates, (11) termite, (12) orator, (13) delude, (14) terminate

WORD PUZZLES 35 (p. 205)

(1) pen, (2) enter, (3) eraser, (4) error, (5) oriole, (6) leaves, (7) essential, (8) allies, (9) estimate, (10) teacher

WORD PUZZLES 36 (p. 206)

(1) blast, (2) stone, (3) never, (4) erase, (5) sewer, (6) error, (7) order, (8) erode, (9) demon, (10) onion

WORD PUZZLES 37 (p. 207)

(1) quack, (2) cable, (3) racer, (4) adder, (5) clear, (6) cuffs, (7) bugle, (8) aches, (9) blind, (10) rajah, (11) hiker, (12) molar, (13) camel, (14) ranch, (15) block

WORD PUZZLES 38 (p. 208)

(1) boast, (2) labor, (3) local, (4) lodge, (5) fleet, (6) wafer, (7) bugle, (8) ether, (9) drill, (10) enjoy, (11) ankle, (12) molar

WORD PUZZLES 39 (p. 209)

(1) a, (2) pa, (3) spa, (4) spat, (5) paste, (6) repast, (7) repeats, (8) separate

WORD PUZZLES 40 (p. 210)

(1) train, (2) robin, (3) uncle, (4) adder, (5) cream, (6) rifle, (7) bigot, (8) ashes, (9) onion, (10) rajah, (11) hiker, (12) color, (13) mumps, (14) canoe

WORD PUZZLES 41 (p. 211)

(1) Anna, (2) reader, (3) devoted, (4) searches, (5) etiquette

WORD PUZZLES 42 (p. 212)

(1) prank, (2) crank, (3) crack, (4) track, (5) trace, (6) brace, (7) brave

WORD PUZZLES 43 (p. 213)

(1) no, (2) owl, (3) last, (4) tiger, (5) racket, (6) trailer, (7) released, (8) dehydrate, (9) expiration, (10) nationality

WORD PUZZLES 44 (p. 214)

(1) ghost, (2) apparition, (3) spirit, (4) vision, (5) demon, (6) phantom, (7) specter

WORD SQUARE PUZZLE 45 (p. 215)

TIGER

WORD SQUARE PUZZLE 46 (p. 216)

HAPPINES

WORD SQUARE PUZZLE 47 (p. 217)

Across: so, sore, or, ore, read, ad, add, ha, hair, hairy, air, airy, rye, yet, nest, to, lid, lids, so, soon, on, foot, nut, or, ore, real, aye, ayes, yes
Down: shelf, she, he, elf, for, or, oar, or, ore, rind, in, do, doe, ere, rest, stay, so, son, on, detour, detours, to, tour, tours, our, ours, to, ton, on, to, onto, toe

WORD SQUARE PUZZLE 48 (p. 218)

Across: scent, cent, enter, terror, err, error, or, cap, ape, cape, pea, pear, ear, are, reel, eel, elm, el, or, an, no, nomad, made, mad, ma, ad, cry, did, den, eye, yea, year, ear, are, aren't, rent, to, drip, rip, ripe, ripen, pen, end, dine, din, in, pal, alp, pit, it, pity, yes, at, on, only, lye, yea, year, ear, door, or, do, ran, an, range, orange, get, no, poor, or, ore
Down: score, scored, core, or, ore, red, pa, pad, ad, carry, car, rat, at, to, too, epic, ice, ceil, ill, lob, near, ear, rap, port, rapport, or, tan, an, any, rein, in,

nap, erode, rode, ode, rod, dent, den, rodent, no, remind, mind, in, go, read, ad, tie, old, eon, on, eons, sat, sate, at, ate, men, mend, end, deer, eerie

WORD SQUARE PUZZLE 49 (p. 220)

Across: salmon, perch, tuna, cod, porpoise, seal, lobster, hake, herring, halibut
Down: squid, whale, eel, crab, octopus, oyster, snail, clam, shark, mussel, scallop, pike, haddock

WORD SQUARE PUZZLE 50 (p. 221)

Across: fern, begonia, almond, tulip, maple, palm, violet, cactus, rose, carnation, daisy, hyacinth, birch, chive, dandelion
Down: chrysanthemum, bluebell, zebra, pachysandra, snapdragon, petunia, avocado, lily, elm, oak, orchid, lilacs, beech, pear, aster, gladiolus, iris, poplar, pine, cloudberry, ash

WORD SQUARE PUZZLE 51 (p. 222)

Across: overdrawn, draft, loan, mortgage, interest, bank, time
Down: sum, money, bonds, standard, borrow, borrower, exchange, change, cash, liability, debt, check, checkbook, arrears, asset, savings, credit, creditor

WORD SQUARE PUZZLE 52 (p. 223)

Across: tea, teach, each, ache, he, her, teacher, ho hold, old, dale, ale, enter, ha, be, bee, eel, write, rite, it, rid, ride, idea, deal, ideal
Down: theater, the, he, heat, heater, eat, at, ate, eater, eon, on, one, new, ewe, we, alter, tar, are, red, debit, bit, it, bite, ha, hare, are, tea, he, heel, eel, real, realtor, alto, or

WORD SQUARE PUZZLE 53 (p. 224)

(intelligent—word in vertical center)
Across: bright, knowing, keen, alert, clever, wise, sage, expert, ingenious, adroit, sharp
Down: sapient, dexterous, shrewd, deft, brilliant, smart, prudent

WORD RECTANGLE PUZZLE 54 (p. 225)

Across: cat, pig, hamster, spider, rooster, rabbit, hog, peacock, moose, eel, elephant, ant, tiger, horse, boa, boar, ram, cow, worm, eagle, toad, swan, bee, giraffe, frog, turkey, ocelot
Down: rhinoceros, salmon, ape, penguin, sheep, bat, goat, dog, goose, rat, asp, crab, seal, fox, ox, wasp, hornet, lion, fly, crow, lamb, shark

WORD RECTANGLE PUZZLE 55 (p. 226)

Across: people, doors, kitchen, floors, sheets, television, sofa, fan, food, pots, clock, stove, oven, pillows, lamp, pictures, steps, cot, refrigerator,
Down: closets, drapes, pets, mirrors, plants, bed, bedroom, lamps, sink, den, rug, books, window, couch, chairs, radio, desk

WORD RIDDLE PUZZLE 56 (p. 227)

(1) dread—read—d; (2) ideal—deal—i; (3) narrow—arrow—n; (4) orange—range—o; (5) scar—car—s; (6) atom—Tom—a; (7) unit—nit—u; (8) race—ace—r; (9) dinosaur

WORD RIDDLE PUZZLE 57 (p. 228)

river

WORD RIDDLE PUZZLE 58 (p. 229)

candle

WORD RIDDLE PUZZLE 59 (p. 230)

carpet

WORD RIDDLE PUZZLE 60 (p. 231)

mistletoe

WORD RIDDLE PUZZLE 61 (p. 232)

firefly

WORD RIDDLE PUZZLE 62 (p. 233)

caterpillar

WORD RIDDLE PUZZLE 63 (p. 234)

fence

WORD RIDDLE PUZZLE 64 (p. 235)

pepper

WORD RIDDLE PUZZLE 65 (p. 236)

at the zoo

RHYMING WORD PUZZLES 66 (p. 237)

(1) liar, (2) fire, (3) tire, (4) higher, (5) wire, (6) dryer, (7) fryer, (8) choir, (9) hire, (10) mire, (11) sire, (12) dire

RHYMING WORD PUZZLES 67 (p. 238)

(1) nine, (2) pine, (3) swine, (4) mine, (5) wine, (6) shine, (7) fine, (8) dine, (9) twine, (10) line, (11) sign, (12) Rhine, (13) brine, (14) vine

RHYMING WORD PUZZLES 68 (p. 239)

(1) bout, (2) route, (3) doubt, (4) drought, (5) pout, (6) lout, (7) gout

RHYMING WORD PUZZLES 69 (p. 240)

(1) bad lad, (2) silly filly, (3) butter cutter, (4) crepe drape, (5) droll troll

RHYMING WORD PUZZLES 70 (p. 241)

(1) fat rat, (2) frail male, (3) rare hare, (4) mad cad, (5) wild child, (6) fender bender

RHYMING WORD PUZZLES 71 (p. 242)

(1) funny bunny, (2) book crook, (3) loud crowd, (4) fair share, (5) sore bore

RHYMING WORD PUZZLES 72 (p. 243)

(1) wet pet, (2) gal pal, (3) major wager, (4) tame game, (5) critter litter, (6) limp shrimp

SCRAMBLED WORD PUZZLES 73 (p. 244)

(1) goat, cow; (2) purple, red; (3) daisy, rose; (4) peach, grape; (5) ant, wasp; (6) bean, pea; (7) tiger, bear; (8) pine, maple; (9) canary, lark; (10) flounder, oyster

SCRAMBLED WORD PUZZLES 74 (p. 245)

(1) cat, dog; (2) pigeon, robin; (3) wolf, gorilla; (4) spider, tick; (5) tulip, violet; (6) willow, maple; (7) trout, cod; (8) pineapple, apple

SCRAMBLED WORD PUZZLES 75 (p. 246)

(1) nap, (2) won, (3) ten, (4) east, (5) tale, (6) mane, (7) tar, (8) arc, (9) Rome, (10) earn, (11) bale, (12) pore, (13) reap, (14) nape, (15) ban

SCRAMBLED WORD PUZZLES 76 (p. 255)

(1) saw, (2) seal, (3) plum, (4) lead, (5) laps, (6) Nile, (7) file, (8) scent, (9) swear, (10) vile

SCRAMBLED WORD PUZZLES 77 (p. 256)

(1) sick, (2) blue, (3) dime, (4) milk, (5) hail, (6) sand, (7) mare, (8) bank, (9) rose, (10) fair, (11) tray, (12) dove, (13) aide, (14) rice, (15) wasp

SCRAMBLED WORD PUZZLES 78 (p. 257)

(1) crow, (2) wasp, (3) wolf, (4) tuna, (5) Peru

SCRAMBLED WORD PUZZLES 79 (p. 258)

(1) east, (2) pail, (3) ease, (4) rear, (5) echo, (6) mink, (7) reef

SCRAMBLED WORD PUZZLES 80 (p. 259)

(1) please, (2) priest, (3) mariner, (4) sacred, (5) legal, (6) ridge, (7) divide

SCRAMBLED WORD PUZZLES 81 (p. 260)

(1) toad, frog; (2) oyster, mussel; (3) nutmeg, pepper; (4) mold, algae; (5) loon, hawk; (6) snake, crocodile; (7) rhinoceros, elephant

SCRAMBLED WORD PUZZLES 82 (p. 261)

(1) dairy, (2) dank, (3) trial, (4) wane, (5) wince, (6) rude, (7) order

SCRAMBLED WORD PUZZLES 83 (p. 262)

(1) stream, (2) notice, (3) reveal, (4) malice, (5) prance, (6) rancid

SCRAMBLED WORD PUZZLES 84 (p. 263)

(1) brave, (2) fearless, (3) bold, (4) courageous, (5) unafraid, (6) daring, (7) plucky, (8) valiant, (9) gallant, (10) undaunted, (11) intrepid, (12) unintimidated, (13) dauntless

HIDDEN WORD PUZZLES 85 (p. 264)

(1) cape—ape; (2) beard—bear; (3) catcher—cat; (4) pearl—pear; (5) peel—eel; (6) cram—ram; (7) camel Liar—camellia; (8) high yen and—hynea; (9) prestige remains—tiger; (10) low aspirations—wasp; asp

HIDDEN WORD PUZZLES 86 (p. 247)

(1) cap exploded—ape, (2) burro seemed—rose, (3) a Siamese—Asia, (4) thief Al confessed—falcon, (5) Tom, at our—tomato, (6) buff a long—Buffalo, (7) we edited—weed, (8) A dam should—Adams

HIDDEN WORD PUZZLES 87 (p. 248)

(1) moth—Mother; (2) maple—Grandma Pleasant; (3) east—sea story; (4) orange—nor angel; (5) panther—pan there

HIDDEN WORD PUZZLES 88 (p. 249)

(1) Washing tons—Washington; (2) main event—Maine; (3) India, Nancy—Indiana; (4) but a house—Utah; (5) Al ask a—Alaska; (6) florid animal—Florida; (7) more go now—Oregon

HIDDEN WORD PUZZLES 89 (p. 250)

(1) beagle—eagle; (2) Clark—lark; (3) Now, let's—owl; (4) Then—hen; (5) crab at—bat; (6) Shaw King—hawk; (7) fairy's wand—swan; (8) throb in—robin; (9) card in Alan's—cardinal; (10) her on—heron

HIDDEN WORD PUZZLES 90 (p. 251)

(1) spa in—Spain, (2) am Erica, a—America, (3) can a dark—Canada, (4) den Mark—Denmark, (5) fin landed—Finland, (6) hit Al yesterday—Italy, (7) chin and—China, (8) often glands—England, (9) tigerman yelled—Germany, (10) dice landed—Iceland

HIDDEN CLUE PUZZLES 91 (p. 252)

(1) hands, (2) handkerchief, (3) candy, (4) land, (5) bandage, (6) bank, (7) bang, (8) plant, (9) airplane, (10) wander, (11) assistant, (12) planet

HIDDEN CLUE PUZZLES 92 (p. 253)

(1) hate, (2) plate, (3) mate, (4) late, (5) gate, (6) date, (7) state, (8) create, (9) imitate, (10) estate, (11) deflate, (12) originate, (13) separate, (14) estimate, (15) demonstrate

HIDDEN CLUE PUZZLES 93 (p. 254)

(1) ant, (2) pants, (3) plants, (4) infant, (5) elephant, (6) tyrant, (7) assistant, (8) fragrant, (9) pleasant, (10) fantasy, (11) chant, (12) slant, (13) antenna, (14) antelope, (15) tantrum, (16) lantern, (17) want, (18) Grant, (19) gallant, (20) nonchalant

HIDDEN CLUE PUZZLES 94 (p. 265)

(1) cage, (2) page, (3) wages, (4) garage, (5) luggage, (6) manage, (7) carriage, (8) rage, (9) sage, (10) wattage

HIDDEN CLUE PUZZLES 95 (p. 266)

(1) halt, (2) salt, (3) malted, (4) Walt, (5) alternate, (6) Baltimore, (7) altitude, (8) alter, (9) alto, (10) malt, (11) altar, (12) altogether, (13) halter, (14) falter, (15) altruist

HIDDEN CLUE PUZZLES 96 (p. 267)

(1) plant—ant; (2) crown—crow ; (3) slice—lice; (4) beard—bear; (5) heel—eel; (6) numerator—rat; (7) gram—ram; (8) toxic—ox; (9) beep—bee; (10) molecule—mole

HIDDEN CLUE PUZZLES 97 (p. 268)

(1) price—rice; (2) beetle—beet; (3) peace—pea; (4) plume—plum; (5) scream—cream; (6) pierce—pie; (7) nutrition—nut; (8) spear—pear; (9) candidate—date; (10) fight—fig

HIDDEN CLUE PUZZLES 98 (p. 269)

(1) grape—ape; (2) camel—camellia; (3) adder—ladder; (4) owl—fowl; (5) cat—catalog; (6) ox—box; (7) ant—slant; (8) hen—Athens; (9) pig—spigot; (10) dog—dogma

HIDDEN CLUE PUZZLES 99 (p. 270)

(1) palace, (2) palm, (3) palate, (4) principal, (5) palpitate, (6) paltry, (7) impale

HIDDEN CLUE PUZZLES 100 (p. 271)

(1) cape, (2) caper, (3) capacity, (4) capitol, (5) captive, (6) capillary, (7) capitulate, (8) capricious

Student Self-Evaluation Progress Report

Student's Name _____

Fun with Words

Riddle or Puzzle Number	Date	Number Correct/Possible Number Correct*
Word Riddles 1		(8)
Word Riddles 2		(10)
Word Riddles 3		(15)
Word Riddles 4		(14)
Word Riddles 5		(20)
Word Riddles 6		(10)
Word Riddles 7		(10)
Word Riddles 8		(10)
Word Riddles 9		(13)
Word Riddles 10		(8)
Word Riddles 11		(8)
Word Riddles 12		(12)
Word Riddles 13		(12)
Word Riddles 14		(12)
Word Riddles 15		(10)
Word Riddles 16		(12)
Word Riddles 17		(8)
Word Riddles 18		(10)
Word Riddles 19		(4)
Word Riddles 20		(4)
Word Puzzles 21		(8)
Word Puzzles 22		(10)
Word Puzzles 23		(15)
Word Puzzles 24		(16)
Word Puzzles 25		(11)
Word Puzzles 26		(10)
Word Puzzles 27		(15)
Word Puzzles 28		(14)
Word Puzzles 29		(11)
Word Puzzles 30		(15)

*If a specific word riddle has two or three parts to its answer, this would be considered as two or three possible numbers correct rather than just one.

Riddle or Puzzle Number	Date	Number Correct/ Possible Number Correct*
Word Puzzles 31		(10)
Word Puzzles 32		(11)
Word Puzzles 33		(12)
Word Puzzles 34		(14)
Word Puzzles 35		(10)
Word Puzzles 36		(10)
Word Puzzles 37		(15)
Word Puzzles 38		(12)
Word Puzzles 39		(8)
Word Puzzles 40		(14)
Word Puzzles 41		(5)
Word Puzzles 42		(7)
Word Puzzles 43		(10)
Word Puzzles 44		(7)
Word Square Puzzle 45		(6)
Word Square Puzzle 46		(10)
Word Square Puzzle 47		(61)
Word Square Puzzle 48		(131)
Word Square Puzzle 49		(23)
Word Square Puzzle 50		(36)
Word Square Puzzle 51		(25)
Word Square Puzzle 52		(59)
Word Square Puzzle 53		(18)
Word Rectangle Puzzle 54		(49)
Word Rectangle Puzzle 55		(36)
Word Riddle Puzzle 56		(17)
Word Riddle Puzzle 57		(6)
Word Riddle Puzzle 58		(7)
Word Riddle Puzzle 59		(7)
Word Riddle Puzzle 60		(10)
Word Riddle Puzzle 61		(8)
Word Riddle Puzzle 62		(12)
Word Riddle Puzzle 63		(6)
Word Riddle Puzzle 64		(7)
Word Riddle Puzzle 65		(9)
Rhyming Word Puzzle 66		(12)
Rhyming Word Puzzle 67		(14)

Student's Name _____

Riddle or Puzzle Number	Date	Number Correct/ Possible Number Correct*
Rhyming Word Puzzle 68		(7)
Rhyming Word Puzzles 69		(10)
Rhyming Word Puzzles 70		(12)
Rhyming Word Puzzles 71		(10)
Rhyming Word Puzzles 72		(12)
Scrambled Word Puzzles 73		(20)
Scrambled Word Puzzles 74		(16)
Scrambled Word Puzzles 75		(15)
Scrambled Word Puzzles 76		(10)
Scrambled Word Puzzles 77		(15)
Scrambled Word Puzzles 78		(5)
Scrambled Word Puzzles 79		(7)
Scrambled Word Puzzles 80		(7)
Scrambled Word Puzzles 81		(7)
Scrambled Word Puzzles 82		(7)
Scrambled Word Puzzles 83		(6)
Scrambled Word Puzzles 84		(13)
Hidden Word Puzzles 85		(10)
Hidden Word Puzzles 86		(8)
Hidden Word Puzzles 87		(5)
Hidden Word Puzzles 88		(7)
Hidden Word Puzzles 89		(10)
Hidden Word Puzzles 90		(10)
Hidden Clue Puzzles 91		(12)
Hidden Clue Puzzles 92		(15)
Hidden Clue Puzzles 93		(20)
Hidden Clue Puzzles 94		(10)
Hidden Clue Puzzles 95		(15)
Hidden Clue Puzzles 96		(10)
Hidden Clue Puzzles 97		(10)
Hidden Clue Puzzles 98		(10)
Hidden Clue Puzzles 99		(7)
Hidden Clue Puzzles 100		(8)

Other time-saving tools for busy teachers by Dorothy Rubin...

THE PRIMARY-GRADE TEACHER'S LANGUAGE ARTS HANDBOOK

and

THE INTERMEDIATE-GRADE TEACHER'S LANGUAGE ARTS HANDBOOK

Make language arts fun for your students—and easier for you to teach—with Dorothy Rubin's two new language arts handbooks. They will help students to improve their language arts skills—listening, speaking, reading, and writing. The handbooks include:

● Numerous enjoyable exercises at graduated ability levels that are intended to be duplicated for use in your class so that the students can work independently.

● Practical lesson plans for each language arts area.

● Challenging activities to capture student interest.

● Diagnostic checklist for assessing the students' needs and progress.

● A detailed outline showing where to find activities that meet specific needs.

Rubin's handbooks give you all the materials necessary for building a stimulating and rewarding language arts program.

For all of you who use and enjoy Lee Bennett Hopkins' monthly feature in Teacher magazine...

THE BEST OF BOOK BONANZA

An extensive collection, adaptation, and update of Hopkins' columns are contained in this one convenient volume. Hopkins not only provides a reliable and sensitive reference of children's literature (from elementary to junior high school) but also synthesizes his commentary into a teaching format so well that he gives teachers a natural springboard for ideas. All of the numerous activities and ideas in *The Best of Book Bonanza* have proven successful for increasing creativity and classroom interest throughout the country.

The best book yet on classroom discipline, by Laurel Tanner. . .

CLASSROOM DISCIPLINE FOR EFFECTIVE TEACHING AND LEARNING

Tanner persuasively argues that in a democratic society the goal of discipline is self-direction. With this in mind, she presents discipline as a sequence of developmental stages and explains how you can help your students direct their energies toward constructive learning goals.

"For administrators who wish to move from the rapped knuckles, external control type of discipline to that which is internal and thus self-directed, this down-to-earth presentation will be a happy discovery."

NASSP Bulletin

M. Jansen/Special Sales
Holt, Rinehart and Winston
P. O. Box 3699
383 Madison Avenue
New York, New York 10017

PAYMENT ENCLOSED plus 5% of list price for shipping, $ .75 for handling, and applicable sales tax. **Payment must accompany your order unless it is placed on your organization's official purchase order form.** In that instance *only*, we will bill you. Please make payment by check or money order payable to Holt, Rinehart and Winston. If we receive your payment but cannot ship within 30 days, full payment will be refunded. If after 30 days you are dissatisfied with your book(s) for any reason, return it (them) to us in saleable condition for a full refund.

_____ 1. Rubin, *The Primary-Grade Teacher's Language Arts Handbook*
0-03-053776-2 $14.95   spiral bound
_____ 2. Rubin, *The Intermediate-Grade Teacher's Language Arts Handbook*
0-03-053781-9 $14.95   spiral bound
_____ 3. Hopkins, *The Best of Book Bonanza*
0-03-056714-9 $13.95   cloth
_____ 4. Tanner, *Classroom Discipline for Effective Teaching and Learning*
0-03-041631-0 $13.95   cloth

Name_____

Affiliation_____

Address_____

City_____ State_____ Zip_____

Your Signature_____ Date_____

4/80   RUB

Prices subject to change without notice

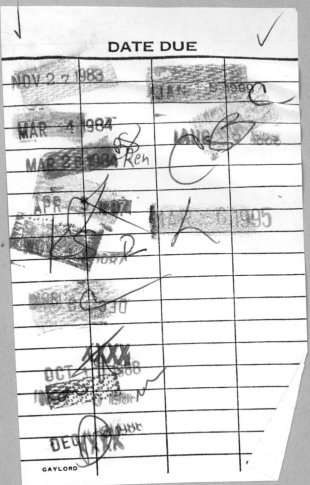

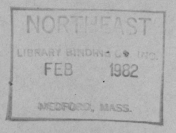